go! CHINESE

聽說讀打寫

Go 100

Textbook
(Traditional Character Edition)

羅秋昭
Julie LO

薛意梅
Emily YIH

CENGAGE Learning

Andover • Melbourne • Mexico City • Stamford, CT • Toronto • Hong Kong • New Delhi • Seoul • Singapore • Tokyo

CENGAGE
Learning®

Go! Chinese Go100 Textbook
(Traditional Character Edition)

Julie Lo, Emily Yih

Publishing Director:
Roy Lee

Editorial Manager, CLT:
Lan Zhao

Development Editor:
Coco Koh

Senior Product Manager (Asia):
Joyce Tan

Product Manager (Outside Asia):
Mei Yun Loh

Regional Manager, Production & Rights:
Pauline Lim

Production Executive:
Evan Wu

For product information and technology assistance, contact us at
Cengage Learning Asia Customer Support, 65-6410-1200

For permission to use material from this text or product,
submit all requests online at **www.cengageasia.com/permissions**
Further permission questions can be emailed to
asia.permissionrequest@cengage.com

ISBN-13: 978-981-4226-88-2
ISBN-10: 981-4226-88-2

Cengage Learning Asia Pte Ltd
151 Lorong Chuan
#02-08 New Tech Park
Singapore 556741

Cengage Learning is a leading provider of customized learning solutions with office locations around the globe, including Andover, Melbourne, Mexico City, Stamford (CT), Toronto, Hong Kong, New Delhi, Seoul, Singapore, and Tokyo. Locate your local office at **www.cengage.com/global**

Cengage Learning products are represented in Canada by Nelson Education, Ltd.

For product information, visit **www.cengageasia.com**

Photo credits:
Cover: © Charly Franklin/Taxi/Getty Images. p.28: (left to right) 31210800, 36107311, 23299479, 231420920, 2701148 © Jupiterimages Corporation; p.38: 36107095 © Jupiterimages Corporation.

Printed in Taiwan
16 17 18 17 16 15 14

Acknowledgements

Go! Chinese is designed to be used together with *IQChinese Go* courseware, a series of multimedia CD-ROM developed by **IQChinese**. We sincerely thank **Wu, Meng-Tien** (Instruction Manager, IQChinese) and **Lanni Wang** (Instruction Specialist, IQChinese) for their tremendous editorial support and advice throughout the development of this program.

We also like to thank the following individuals who offered many helpful insights, ideas, and suggestions for improvement during the product development stage of *Go! Chinese*.

- **Jessie Lin Brown**, Singapore American School, Singapore
- **Henny Chen**, Moreau Catholic High School, USA
- **Yeafen Chen**, University of Wisconsin-Milwaukee, USA
- **Christina Hsu**, Superior Education, USA
- **Yi Liang Jiang**, Beijing Language and Culture University, China
- **Yan Jin**, Singapore American School, Singapore
- **Kerman Kwan**, Irvine Chinese School, USA
- **Andrew Scrimgeour**, University of South Australia, Australia
- **James L. Tan**, Grace Christian High School, the Philippines
- **Man Tao**, Koning Williem I College, the Netherlands
- **Chiungwen Tsai**, Westside Chinese School, USA
- **Tina Wu**, Westside High School, USA
- **YaWen (Alison) Yang**, Concordian International School, Thailand

Preface

Go! Chinese, together with *IQChinese Go* **multimedia CD-ROM**, is a fully-integrated Chinese language program that offers an easy, enjoyable, and effective learning experience for learners of Chinese as a foreign language.

The themes and lesson plans of this program are designed with references to the American National Standards for Foreign Language Learning developed by ACTFL[1], and the Curriculum Guides for Modern Languages developed by the Toronto District Board of Education. The program aims to help beginners develop their communicative competence in the four language skills of listening, speaking, reading, and writing while gaining an appreciation of the Chinese culture, exercising their ability to compare and contrast different cultures, making connections with other discipline areas, and extending their learning experiences to their homes and communities.

The program employs innovative teaching methodologies and computer applications to enhance language learning, as well as keep students motivated in and outside of the classroom. The companion CD-ROM gives students access to audio, visual, and textual information about the language all at once. Chinese typing is systematically integrated into the program to facilitate the acquisition and retention of new vocabulary and to equip students with a skill that is becoming increasingly important in the Internet era wherein more and more professional and personal correspondence are done electronically.

Course Design

The program is divided into two series: Beginner and Intermediate. The Beginner Series, which comprises four levels (Go100-400), provides a solid foundation for continued study of the Intermediate Series (Go500-800). Each level includes a student text, a workbook, and a companion CD-ROM.

Beginner Series: Go100 – Go400

Designed for zero beginners, each level of the Beginner Series is made up of 10 colorfully illustrated lessons. Each lesson covers new vocabulary and simple sentence structures with particular emphasis on listening and speaking skills. In keeping with the communicative approach, a good mix of activities such as role play, interviews, games, pair work, and language exchanges are incorporated to allow students to learn to communicate through interaction in the target language. The CD-ROM uses rhythmic chants, word games, quizzes, and Chinese typing exercises to improve students' pronunciation, mastery of *pinyin*, and their ability to recognize and read words and sentences taught in each lesson.

The Beginner Series can be completed in roughly 240 hours (160 hours on Textbook and 80 hours on CD-ROM). Upon completion of the Beginner Series, the student will have acquired approximately 500 Chinese characters and 1000 common phrases.

Intermediate Series: Go500 – Go800

The Intermediate Series continues with the use of the communicative approach, but places a greater emphasis on Culture, Community, and Comparison. Through stories revolving around Chinese-American families, students learn vocabulary necessary for expressing themselves in a variety of contexts, describing their world, and discussing cultural differences.

The Intermediate Series can be completed in roughly 320 hours (240 hours on Textbook and 80 hours on CD-ROM). Upon completion of both the Beginner and Intermediate Series, the student will have acquired approximately 1000 Chinese characters and 2400 common phrases.

[1] American Council on the Teaching of Foreign Languages (http://www.actfl.org)

Vocabulary and Sentence Structures

The program places emphasis on helping students use the target language in contexts relevant to their everyday lives. Therefore, the chosen vocabulary and sentence structures are based on familiar topics such as family, school activities, hobbies, weather, shopping, food, pets, modes of transport, etc. The same topics are revisited throughout the series to reinforce learning, as well as to expand on the vocabulary and sentence structures acquired before.

Listening and Speaking

Communicative activities encourage and require a learner to speak with and listen to other learners. Well-designed and well-executed communicative activities can help turn the language classroom into an active and enjoyable place where learners are motivated to learn and can learn what they need. The program integrates a variety of communicative activities such as role play, interviews, games, pair work, and language exchanges to give students the opportunity to put what they have learned into practice.

Word Recognition and Reading

Each lesson introduces about 12 new Chinese characters. Using the spiral approach, each new character is first introduced and then recycled in classroom activities and subsequent lessons to enhance retention of new vocabulary over time. *Pinyin* (phonetic notation) is added above newly introduced characters so that students can learn to pronounce them. To make sure students do not become over-reliant on *pinyin* to read Chinese, recycled vocabulary is stripped of *pinyin* so that students can learn to recognize and read the actual written characters in due course. For the same reason, the companion CD-ROM does not display the *pinyin* of words automatically.

Type-to-Learn Methodology

The unique characteristic of this series is the use of Chinese typing as an instructional strategy to improve listening, pronunciation, and word recognition. Activities in the CD-ROM require students to type characters or sentences as they are read aloud or displayed on the computer screen. Students will be alerted if they make a mistake and will be given the chance to correct them. If they do not get it right on the third try, the software provides immediate feedback on how to correct the error. This interactive trial-and-error method allows students to develop self-confidence and learn the language by doing.

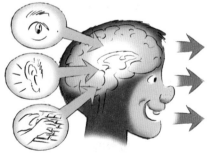

TYPE Chinese characters with the 26 letters of the alphabet

HEAR Chinese words read aloud

SEE the correct Chinese character

USE multiple senses to learn

Chinese Characters and Character Writing

The program does not require the student to be able to hand-write all the core vocabulary; the teacher may however assign more character writing practice according to his or her classroom emphasis and needs. What the program aims to do is to give students a good grasp of Chinese radicals and stroke order rules, as well as to help students understand and appreciate the characteristics and formation of Chinese characters. The program includes writing practice on frequently used characters. Understanding the semantic function radicals have in the characters they form and having the ability to see compound characters by their simpler constituents enable students to memorize new characters in a logical way.

Using the CD-ROM as an Instructional Aid

The following diagram shows how a teacher might use the CD-ROM as an instructional aid to improve traditional classroom instruction.

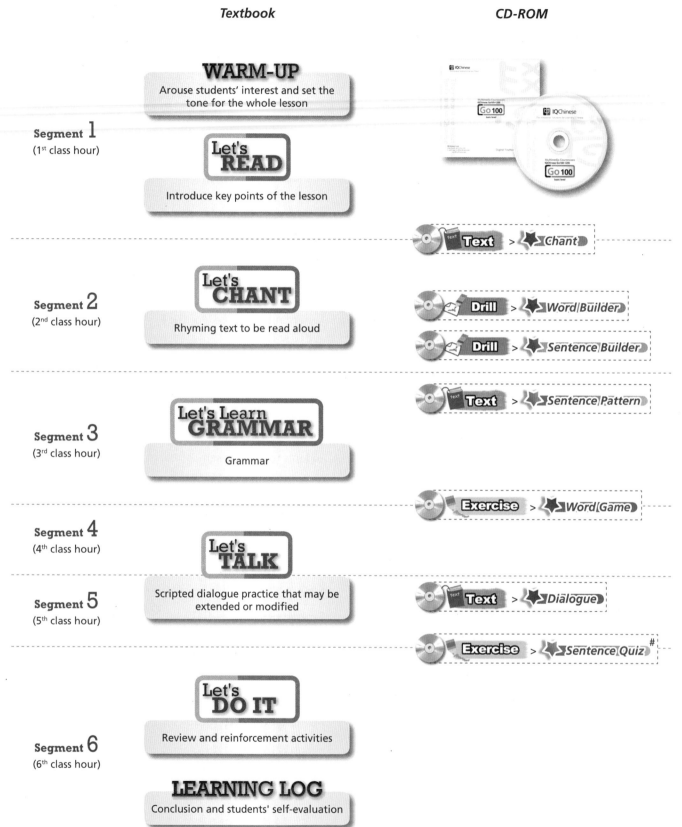

#Sentence Quiz Exercise

The section *Exercise > Sentence Quiz* in the CD-ROM enhances learning by stimulating multiple senses and providing immediate feedback on students' performance.

The Sentence Quiz exercise comprises four levels.

- Level 1 – Warm-up Quiz (Look, Listen, and Type): Chinese text, *pinyin*, and audio prompts are provided.
- Level 2 – Visual-aid Quiz: Only Chinese text is provided. There are no *pinyin* or audio prompts.
- Level 3 – Audio-aid Quiz: Only audio prompts are provided.
- Level 4 – Character-selection Quiz: Only Chinese text is provided. After entering the correct *pinyin*, students are required to select the correct character from a list of similar-looking characters.

Classroom Setup and Equipment

For small classes (up to 5 students), the teacher can show the CD-ROM features on one computer with students gathered around the screen. For large groups, a projector will be needed to project the computer's display onto a large screen so that the entire class can see.

If the classroom is not equipped with computers, the teacher may have students bring their own portable computers to class so that they can work individually or in small groups of 2 to 3 on the CD-ROM activities during designated class hours. CD-ROM activities may also be assigned as homework.

Suggestions for Teachers

We recommend that teachers

- be flexible in using the *pinyin* unit. They may, for example, extend the *pinyin* exercise to an enunciation exercise based on the lesson's theme and new vocabulary. They may also choose to use the *pinyin* unit as an introductory exercise before embarking on the first lesson of the series.
- spend 4-5 hours on each lesson in the Textbook and 2 hours on each lesson in the CD-ROM. The course materials and lesson length may be adjusted according to students' proficiency level and learning ability.
- allocate 1-2 class hours to go over with students the Review units in the Workbook as a way to check on the students' progress.
- have students complete 1-2 pages of the Workbook after every two class sessions.
- encourage students to spend 10 minutes a day on the Sentence Quiz in the CD-ROM. Practice makes perfect!

More Support

IQChinese is the publisher for *IQChinese Go* multimedia CD-ROMs. By adopting Type-To-Learn as its core methodology, IQChinese provides learners of the Chinese language a complete solution to learn the language effectively.

Courseware & Homework

- "Type-to-Learn" courseware for PC & Mac
- textbook & workbook
- online practice system
- mobile practice apps for iOS
- Chinese learning software

Teaching Support

- online teaching resources
- teacher training & workshops
- supporting software

Technical Support

- product installation
- school site license
- digital learning conversion
- digital teaching planning

Scope & Sequence

Lesson	Communicative Goals	Vocabulary	Language Usage	Cultural Information
一二三 **One Two Three** **1**	• Count up to 100 • Indicate the count of an item	**Numbers 1 to 100** 一, 二… 十, 百, 兩, 個	• **Usage of "二" and "兩"** 二十, 兩百, 一千二百 • **Measure word "個"** 一個, 兩個	
你好嗎？ **How Are You?** **2**	• Greet people in different situations • Ask how someone is doing	**Greetings** 你, 我, 他, 你們, 大家, 好, 嗎, 很, 早, 再見…	• **Personal pronouns** 你, 我, 他 • **Plural form of personal pronouns** 我們, 你們, 他們 • **Modulation of third-tone words** 你好, 你早, 很好 • **Interrogative sentence with "嗎"** 你好嗎？	• How Chinese people greet one another
謝謝你！ **Thank You!** **3**	• Express and respond to a thank-you • Express and respond to an apology	**Thanks and Apologies** 謝謝, 不客氣, 對不起, 沒關係, 請, 不用…	• **Usage of "謝謝" and "不客氣"** 謝謝大家, 請不用客氣 • **Adverb "不" and negative form** 不好, 不對, 不用謝	• Chinese characters with left/right components • Chinese radicals
姓什麼？ **What Is Your Last Name?** **4**	• Ask for someone's name • Tell your name • Introduce others	**Exchanging Names** 請問, 貴姓, 叫, 什麼, 的, 名字, 都…	• **Difference between "姓", "名", and "名字"** 你叫什麼名字？我姓謝，叫小明。 • **Possessive form "的"** 我的名字。 • **Interrogative pronoun "什麼"** 你姓什麼？ 你叫什麼名字？ • **Polite form "請問" when asking questions** 請問你貴姓？	• Chinese names • Common Chinese last names
星期幾？ **What Day Is Today?** **5**	• Express days of the week • Express day, month, and year • Ask and answer questions about dates • Tell the number of days between two given dates	**Dates, months, weeks, years** 星期, 日, 月, 天, 今年, 明年, 去年, 今天, 明天, 昨天, 有, 沒有, 到, 是, 幾, 這個…	• **How to express dates** 今天是二〇〇九年七月十六日星期四。 • **"是" Sentence** 請問今天是幾月幾日？ • **Usage of "到"** 四月一日到四月二十日有二十天。 • **Sentence pattern "有／沒有"** 一個星期有七天。 二月沒有三十日。 • **Usage of "這個"** 這個月有幾個星期？	• Early Chinese writing system: pictograms • Chinese characters with top/bottom components

幾個人？ **How Many People Are There in Your Family?** **6**	• Introduce your family members • Ask about someone's family members • Ask and answer simple yes/no questions	**The Family** 爸爸, 媽媽, 哥哥, 弟弟, 姊姊, 妹妹, 還有, 一共, 人, 口, 家...	• **Measure word "口"** 請問你家幾口人？ • **Sentence patterns "有 / 沒有 / 有……嗎？/ 有沒有……？"** 你有妹妹嗎？我有（沒有）妹妹。 • **Sentence patterns "有……，還有……"** 我有姊姊，還有妹妹。 • **Yes/No questions** 你沒有哥哥嗎？對，我沒有哥哥。	• How to address family members in Chinese
多少錢？ **How Much Is This?** **7**	• Ask what someone wants to buy • Tell someone what you want to buy • Ask for and state the price of an item • Ask for a lower price	**Shopping** 錢, 塊, 要, 買, 那個, 太, 貴, 便宜, 算, 一點兒, 多少...	• **Usage of "這個 / 那個"** 那個十塊錢。 • **Opposites "便宜 / 貴" and "少 / 多"** 27塊太貴了，便宜一點兒好不好？ • **Adverb of degree "很"** 很大, 很小 • **Sentence patterns "要 / 要……嗎？"** 你要買裙子嗎？我不買裙子，我要買鞋子。 • **Usage of "多少 / 幾"** 請問這個多少錢？ 你幾歲？	
幾點鐘？ **What Time Is It?** **8**	• Tell and ask for the time • Ask and tell if someone will be at a certain location at a certain time	**Time Expressions** 點, 分, 半, 鐘, 上午, 中午, 下午, 晚上, 現在, 時, 走, 分鐘...	• **How to tell time** 請問現在幾點（鐘）？現在中午十二點三十五分。 • **Sentence patterns "在 / 不在 / 在……嗎？/ 在不在？"** 明天你在不在家？	
打電話 **Making a Phone Call** **9**	• Conduct basic telephone conversations • Inquire about and tell your telephone number	**Phone Conversation** 打電話, 號, 找, 哪一位, 等, 誰, 來...	• **Usage of "誰"** 請問你找誰？ • **Sentence patterns "是 / 不是 / 是……嗎？"** 他是謝小明嗎？不是，他是小明的哥哥。 • **Usage of "等 / 等一下 / 等一等"** 請你等一等（等一下）。 請你等十分鐘。 • **Difference between "那" and "哪"** 哪一位是小明的爸爸？那位是小明的爸爸。	• Common practice of Chinese people when making or answering phone calls • Chinese radicals
好老師 **A Good Teacher** **10**	• Talk about abilities • Address a teacher politely	**Abilities** 老師, 同學, 教, 學, 中文, 會, 可以, 和, 學生, 有用, 一起...	• **Sentence patterns "會 / 不會 / 會……嗎？"** 你會中文嗎？我會中文。 • **Sentence patterns "可以 / 不可以 / 可以……嗎？"** 我可以打電話嗎？你不可以打電話。	• Chinese refers to someone by their titles as a show of respect for age and hierarchy

Table of Contents

ACKNOWLEDGEMENTS iii

PREFACE iv

SCOPE & SEQUENCE viii

PINYIN 1

LESSON 一二三
1   One Two Three 9

LESSON 你好嗎？
2   How Are You? 19

LESSON 謝謝你！
3   Thank You! 29

LESSON 姓什麼？
4   What Is Your Last Name? 39

LESSON 星期幾？
5   What Day Is Today? 49

LESSON 幾個人？
6   How Many People Are There in Your Family? 61

LESSON 多少錢？
7   How Much Is This? 71

LESSON 幾點鐘？
8   What Time Is It? 81

LESSON 打電話
9   Making a Phone Call 91

LESSON 好老師
10   A Good Teacher 101

VOCABULARY INDEX 111

Pinyin consists of three parts:

Initial + **Final** + **Tone**

Initial	b p m f		d t n l	
	g k h		j q x	
	zh ch sh r		z c s	

Final	a	ai	ao	an	ang
	o	ou			
	e	ei	en	eng	er
	yi (~i)	ya (~ia)	yao (~iao)	yan (~ian)	yang (~iang)
	yo	you (~iu)	ye (~ie)	yin (~in)	ying (~ing)
	wu (~u)	wa (~ua)	wai (~uai)	wan (~uan)	wang (~uang)
	wo (~uo)	wei (~ui)	wen (~un)	weng (~ong)	
	yu (~ü)	yuan (~üan)	yue (~üe)	yun (~ün)	yong (~iong)

| Tone | — 1 | ╱ 2 | ╲ 3 | ╲ 4 |

a o e i u ü

	a	o	e	i	u	ü
b	ba	bo		bi	bu	
m	ma	mo	me	mi	mu	
n	na		ne	ni	nu	nü
l	la		le	li	lu	lü

There are four tones in *pinyin*:

Tone	Tone Mark
1st	—
2nd	╱
3rd	⌄
4th	╲

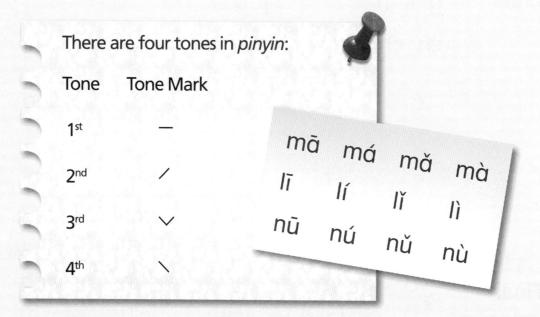

mā má mǎ mà
lī lí lǐ lì
nū nú nǔ nù

bàba

māma

bǐ

lù

nánshēng

nǚshēng

lǜsè

ai ao an ang ei en eng er ou

	ai	ao	an	ang
d	dai	dao	dan	dang
t	tai	tao	tan	tang

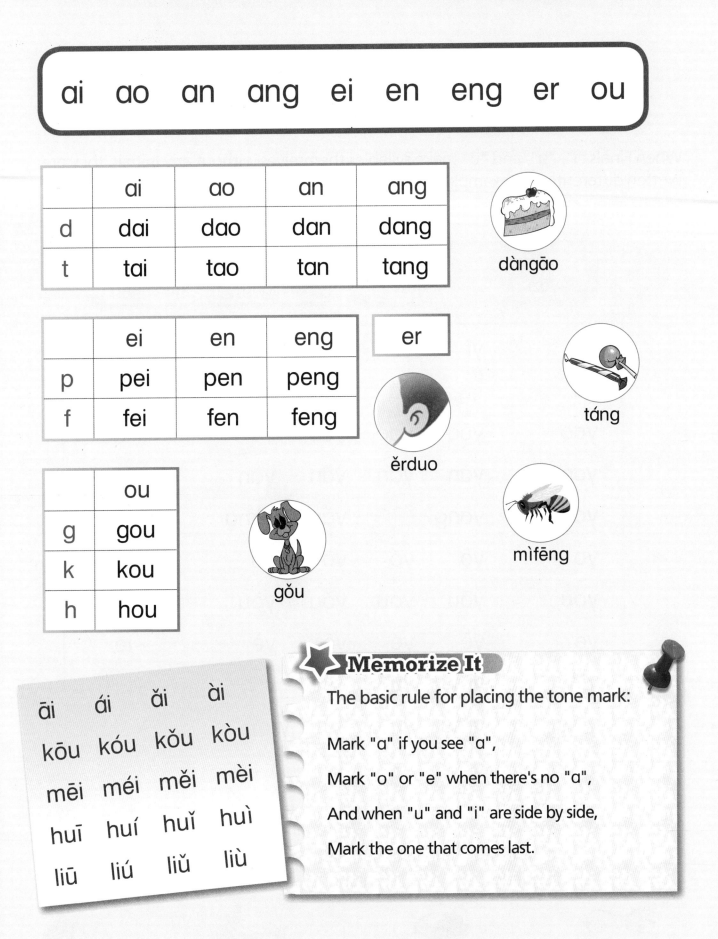

dàngāo

	ei	en	eng
p	pei	pen	peng
f	fei	fen	feng

er

ěrduo

táng

	ou
g	gou
k	kou
h	hou

gǒu

mìfēng

āi   ái   ǎi   ài
kōu kóu kǒu kòu
mēi méi měi mèi
huī huí huǐ huì
liū liú liǔ liù

Memorize It

The basic rule for placing the tone mark:

Mark "a" if you see "a",

Mark "o" or "e" when there's no "a",

And when "u" and "i" are side by side,

Mark the one that comes last.

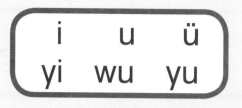

i u ü
yi wu yu

When Finals "i", "u", and "ü" make syllables themselves without any Initials, they are written differently. For example:

yāzi   xiāzi

yuèliàng   xuéshēng

yi	yī	yí	yǐ	yì	~i
ya		yá	yǎ	yà	~ia
yao	yāo	yáo	yǎo		~iao
yan	yān	yán	yǎn	yàn	~ian
yang	yāng		yǎng	yàng	~iang
yo	yō	yó	yǒ	yò	
you	yōu	yóu	yǒu	yòu	~i(o)u
ye	yē	yé	yě	yè	~ie
yin	yīn	yín	yǐn	yìn	~in
ying	yīng	yíng	yǐng	yìng	~ing

diàndēng   niúnǎi   shǒubiǎo

yǎnjīng   miàn   xiāngjiāo   jīnyú

wu	wū	wú	wǔ	wù	~u
wa	wā	wá	wǎ	wà	~ua
wai	wāi	wái	wǎi	wài	~uai
wan	wān	wán	wǎn	wàn	~uan
wang	wāng	wáng	wǎng	wàng	~uang
wo	wō	wó	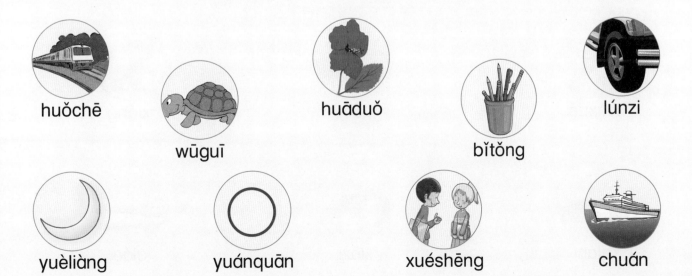	wò	~uo
wei	wēi	wéi	wěi	wèi	~u(e)i
wen	wēn	wén	wěn	wèn	~u(e)n
weng	wēng	wéng	wěng	wèng	~ong

yu	yū		yǔ	yù	~ü
yuan	yuān	yuán	yuǎn	yuàn	~üan
yue	yuē	yué	yuě	yuè	~üe
yun	yūn		yǔn	yùn	~ü(e)n
yong	yōng	yóng	yǒng	yòng	~iong

huǒchē

wūguī

huāduǒ

bǐtǒng

lúnzi

yuèliàng

yuánquān

xuéshēng

chuán

j q x

The Finals "iou", "uei", and "uen" should be written as "iu", "ui", and "un" when they are used with an Initial. For example, "niú", "guī", "lún".

	~i	~ia	~ian	~i(o)u	~ü	~ü(e)n	~iong
j	ji	jia	jian	jiu	ju	jun	jiong
q	qi	qia	qian	qiu	qu	qun	qiong
x	xi	xia	xian	xiu	xu	xun	xiong

The Final "ü" should be written as "u" when it is used with the initials "j", "q", and "x".

xiàxuě

xiǎojī

xióng

qián

xiāzi

qiáo

	ai	e	eng	~u(e)i	~uan	~ong
zh	zhai	zhe	zheng	zhui	zhuan	zhong
ch	chai	che	cheng	chui	chuan	chong
sh	shai	she	sheng	shui	shuan	
r		re	reng	rui	ruan	
z	zai	ze	zeng	zui	zuan	zong
c	cai	ce	ceng	cui	cuan	cong
s	sai	se	seng	sui	suan	song

zh   ch   sh   r   z   c   s
zhi   chi   shi   ri   zi   ci   si

When the Initials "zh", "ch", "sh", "r", "z", "c", and "s" are pronounced alone, they should be written as "zhi", "chi", "shi", "ri", "zi", "ci", and "si".

zhīzhū

shūbāo

shīzi

shízhōng

chuānghù

shūcài

Pinyin **WANT TO LEARN MORE?**

Check out the Pinyin CD.

Let's DO IT

1. Mark the third tone on the *pinyin* and read out the words.

1. yusan

2. shoubiao

3. shuiguo

4. niunai

2. Listen carefully to your teacher. Which item is mentioned?

1. yǎnjīng   yǎnjìng

2. shū   shù

3. Read the sentences.

1. Zǐsè de zhīzhū yǒu jǐ zhī?

2. Gēge kě le hē kělè.

3. Yéye yǒu liù tóu niú.

4. Qī ge qìqiú bǎng yìqǐ.

One Two Three

My Goals

1 Count in Chinese
2 Express the quantity of an item in Chinese
3 Recognize and write Chinese numbers

1	2	3	4	5
yī	èr	sān	sì	wǔ
一	二	三	四	五

yī èr   yī èr sān
一 二   一 二 三

yī èr sān   sān èr yī
一 二 三   三 二 一

yī èr sān sì wǔ
一 二 三 四 五

wǔ sì sān èr yī
五 四 三 二 一

5

4

3

2

1

New Words

yī	èr	sān
一 one	二 two	三 three

sì	wǔ
四 four	五 five

6	7	8	9	10
liù	qī	bā	jiǔ	shí
六	七	八	九	十

yī èr sān　　sān èr yī
一 二 三　　三 二 一

yī èr sān sì wǔ liù qī
一 二 三 四 五 六 七

qī bā jiǔ　　bā jiǔ shí
七 八 九　　八 九 十

qī liù wǔ sì sān èr yī
七 六 五 四 三 二 一

New Words

liù	qī	bā
六 six	七 seven	八 eight

jiǔ	shí
九 nine	十 ten

⭐ Memorize It

Look closely at the roulette and memorize the Chinese numbers 1 to 10.

⭐ Match and Write

Match each number with its corresponding Chinese character. Then fill in the box with the missing Chinese number.

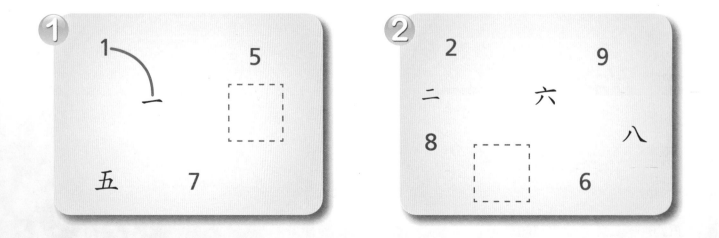

⭐ Challenge Yourself

Count from 1 to 100 in Chinese.

	yī 一	èr 二	sān 三	sì 四	wǔ 五	liù 六	qī 七	bā 八	jiǔ 九
shí 十	shí yī 十一		shí sān 十三		shí wǔ 十五		shí qī 十七		shí jiǔ 十九
èr shí 二十		èr shí èr 二十二		èr shí sì 二十四		èr shí liù 二十六		èr shí bā 二十八	
sān shí 三十		sān shí èr 三十二			sān shí wǔ 三十五		sān shí qī 三十七		sān shí jiǔ 三十九
sì shí 四十			sì shí sān 四十三			sì shí liù 四十六			sì shí jiǔ 四十九
wǔ shí 五十	wǔ shí yī 五十一		wǔ shí sān 五十三		wǔ shí wǔ 五十五		wǔ shí qī 五十七		
liù shí 六十		liù shí èr 六十二		liù shí sì 六十四				liù shí bā 六十八	
qī shí 七十	qī shí yī 七十一			qī shí sì 七十四			qī shí qī 七十七		qī shí jiǔ 七十九
bā shí 八十	bā shí yī 八十一				bā shí wǔ 八十五			bā shí bā 八十八	
jiǔ shí 九十		jiǔ shí èr 九十二		jiǔ shí sì 九十四		jiǔ shí liù 九十六			jiǔ shí jiǔ 九十九
yì bǎi 一百									

New Words

bǎi 百	hundred

Let's CHANT · Go 100

yī èr sān sì wǔ liù qī
一 二 三 四 五 六 七 。

qī liù wǔ sì sān èr yī
七 六 五 四 三 二 一 。

bā shí jiǔ shí yì liǎng bǎi
八 十 、 九 十 、 一 兩 百 。

liù bǎi qī bǎi bā jiǔ bǎi
六 百 、 七 百 、 八 九 百 。

"一兩百" means 100 and 200.

"八九百" means 800 and 900.

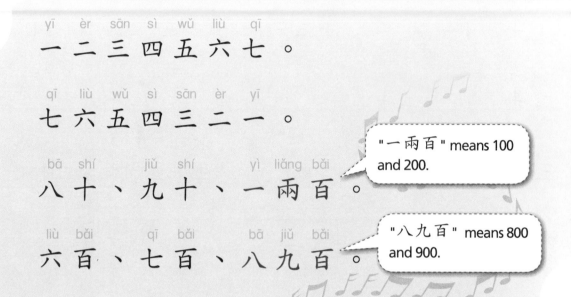

New Words

liǎng
兩 two

1	2	3	4	5	6	7	8	9
yī	èr	sān	sì	wǔ	liù	qī	bā	jiǔ
一	二	三	四	五	六	七	八	九

shí

十

10	20	30	40	50
shí	èr shí	sān shí	sì shí	wǔ shí
十	二十	三十	四十	五十

60	70	80	90
liù shí	qī shí	bā shí	jiǔ shí
六十	七十	八十	九十

bǎi

百

100	200	300	400	500
yì bǎi	liǎng bǎi	sān bǎi	sì bǎi	wǔ bǎi
一百	兩百	三百	四百	五百

600	700	800	900
liù bǎi	qī bǎi	bā bǎi	jiǔ bǎi
六百	七百	八百	九百

TIP

Both "二" and "兩" mean "two", but their usage differs.

❶ We use "兩" before a measure word and noun. For example:

liǎng ge péng yǒu   liǎng ge nǚ shēng
兩個朋友 (two friends)   兩個女生 (two girls)

❷ When counting, "二" must always be used before "十". For example: 二十 (twenty)

❸ When combined with "百", the position of the word affects the usage.

➤ If it is placed at the beginning, we usually say "兩百" (two hundred), although "二百" is also acceptable.

➤ If it is placed in the middle, we usually use "二". For example:

qiān
一千二百二十 (One thousand, two hundred, and twenty)

Let's SING A SONG

shí ge hǎo péng yǒu
十 個 好 朋 友

‖ 1　1　1　1 ｜ 3　5　3 3　1 ｜
yí ge liǎng ge sān ge hǎo péng yǒu
一 個 兩 個 三 個 好 朋 友*，

｜ 2　2　2　2 ｜ 7　2　7 7　5 ｜
sì ge wǔ ge liù ge hǎo péng yǒu
四 個 五 個 六 個 好 朋 友，

｜ 1　1　1　1 ｜ 3　5　3 3　1 ｜
qī ge bā ge jiǔ ge hǎo péng yǒu
七 個 八 個 九 個 好 朋 友，

｜ 2　2　2　5　5 ｜ 1 - - - ‖
shí ge hǎo péng yǒu
十 個 好 朋 友。

*好朋友 good friend

New Words

gè
個 (a measure word, used for objects and people)

TIP

A measure word is used to quantify objects or people (noun). Different nouns require different measure words. "個" is the most commonly used.

	numeral	measure word	noun
Chinese:	我有 兩	個	好朋友。
English:	I have two		good friends.

⭐ **Read Aloud**

yí ge
一 個

liǎng ge
兩 個

sān ge
三 個

sì ge
四 個

wǔ ge
五 個

liù ge
六 個

qī ge
七 個

bā ge
八 個

jiǔ ge
九 個

shí ge
十 個

⭐ **Think and Answer**

Fill in the blanks with the appropriate Chinese number and measure word "個".

1. How many good friends do you have?

wǒ yǒu   hǎo péng yǒu
我 有 _____ 好 朋 友。

2. How many boys and girls are there in your class?

bān shàng yǒu   nán shēng   nǚ shēng
班 上 有 _____ 男 生、_____ 女 生。

Look for the pattern in the charts below. Then write the correct Chinese numbers in the spaces provided.

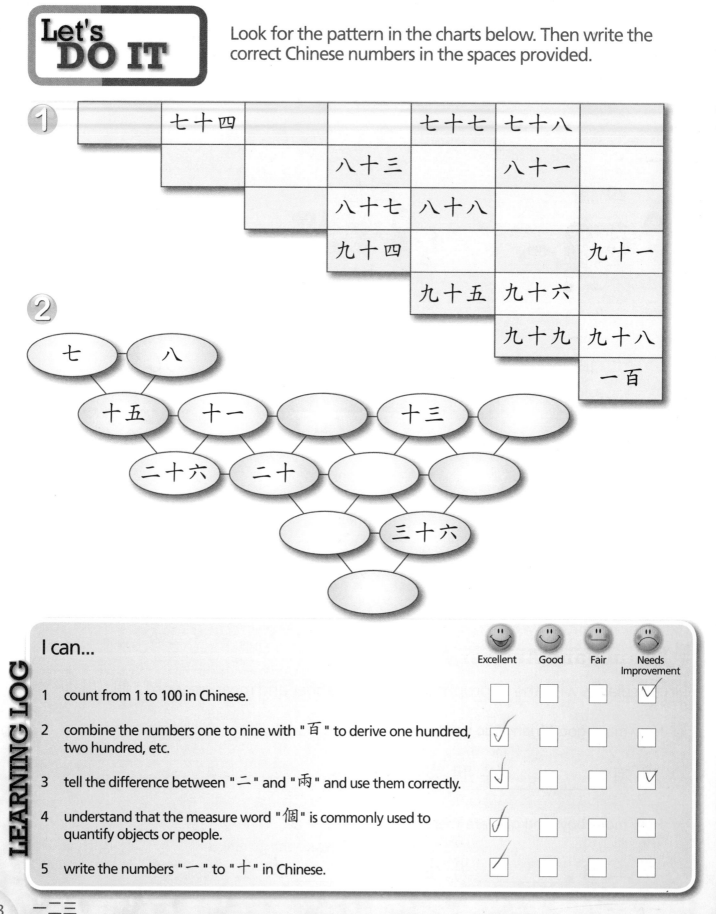

1

	七十四			七十七	七十八	
			八十三		八十一	
			八十七	八十八		
			九十四			九十一
				九十五	九十六	
					九十九	九十八
						一百

2

(七) (八)
(十五) (十一) ( ) (十三) ( )
(二十六) (二十) ( ) ( )
( ) (三十六)
( )

LEARNING LOG

I can...

		Excellent	Good	Fair	Needs Improvement
1	count from 1 to 100 in Chinese.				☑
2	combine the numbers one to nine with "百" to derive one hundred, two hundred, etc.	☑			
3	tell the difference between "二" and "兩" and use them correctly.	☑			☑
4	understand that the measure word "個" is commonly used to quantify objects or people.	☑			
5	write the numbers "一" to "十" in Chinese.	☑			

18   一二三

你好嗎？
How Are You?

My Goals

1　Use appropriate greetings when meeting other people in various situations
2　Respond appropriately to greetings from other people
3　Understand how Chinese people greet each other
4　Recognize and write simple vocabulary associated with greetings

Let's READ

TIP
Besides verbal greetings, Chinese people also use some common gestures or actions to greet each other, such as waving or shaking hands, smiling, and nodding their heads. How do you usually greet your friends?

New Words

你 nǐ you (singular)　　好 hǎo fine; good　　早 zǎo early; morning

你早 nǐ zǎo Good morning (to you)　　你好 nǐ hǎo hello

20　你好嗎？

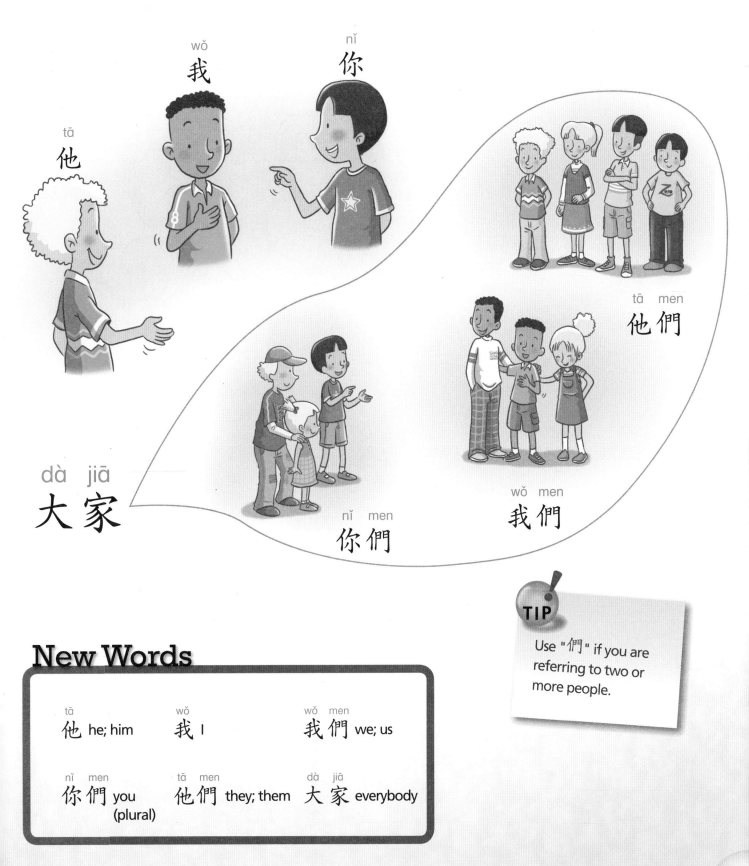

New Words

他 tā he; him

我 wǒ I

我們 wǒ men we; us

你們 nǐ men you (plural)

他們 tā men they; them

大家 dà jiā everybody

nǐ hǎo ma
你 好 嗎 ？

wǒ hěn hǎo
我 很 好 。

tā hǎo ma
他 好 嗎 ？

tā hěn hǎo
他 很 好 ！

nǐ hǎo nǐ hǎo dà jiā hǎo
你 好 ！ 你 好 ！ 大 家 好 ！

nǐ zǎo nǐ zǎo dà jiā zǎo
你 早 ！ 你 早 ！ 大 家 早 ！

New Words

ma
嗎 (used when asking a question)

hěn
很 very

Let's Learn GRAMMAR

zǎo
早

hǎo
好

nǐ zǎo
你早

dà jiā zǎo
大家早

nǐ hǎo
你好

tā hěn hǎo
他很好

wǒ hěn hǎo
我很好

⭐ Read Aloud

我　　wǒ

早　　zǎo

好　　hǎo

你　　nǐ

很　　hěn

nǐ zǎo
你早

hěn hǎo
很好

nǐ hǎo
你好

TIP

When two third tones occur together, the preceding word should be pronounced in the second tone. Look at the examples above and circle the words you pronounced in the second tone.

ma
嗎 ？

hǎo
好

hǎo ma
好 嗎 ？

tā hǎo ma
他 好 嗎 ？

hǎo ma
Tom 好 嗎 ？

tā hǎo ma
Jeff 他 好 嗎 ？

TIP

"嗎 ？ " is an essential component in the interrogative sentence structure. It always appears at the end of a question.

Go100

WANT TO LEARN MORE?

Check out the Text > Sentence Pattern section in the Go100 CD.

Let's TALK

Find a partner and practice the dialogues below.

⭐ Task 1

nǐ hǎo
Tom，你好！

nǐ hǎo
Julie，你好！

tā hǎo ma
Jeff 他好嗎？

tā hěn hǎo
他很好！

⭐ Task 2

nǐ hǎo
Ⓐ：你好！

nǐ hǎo
Ⓑ：你好！

nǐ hǎo ma
Ⓐ：你好嗎？

wǒ hěn hǎo
Ⓑ：我很好。

你好嗎？ 25

Find partners to practice the dialogues below.

Task 3

A : 你們好嗎？
　　nǐ men hǎo ma

B C : 我們很好！
　　　wǒ men hěn hǎo

Task 4

A : 大家早！
　　dà jiā zǎo

B C
D E : 你早！
　　　nǐ zǎo

Go 100

WANT TO LEARN MORE?

Check out the Text > Dialogue section in the Go100 CD.

⭐ Task 5

A 再見！
zài jiàn

B 再見！
zài jiàn

New Words

再見 goodbye
zài jiàn

Bye-bye 再見, bye-bye 再見, see you again!

How do you greet the people in the following situations? Working in pairs, role-play each of the scenarios below.

Scenario 1 You run into your friend outside the classroom in the morning.

Scenario 2 You bump into your old friend, Adam, on the street. You have not seen each other for a long time and wonder how he and his sister, Mary, are doing.

Scenario 3 You run into your classmates who have gathered outside the school library. You are on your way home and bid them goodbye.

LEARNING LOG

I can...

		Excellent	Good	Fair	Needs Improvement
1	exchange simple greetings politely in Chinese.				✓
2	ask how someone is doing.			✓	
3	reply when someone asks me how I am doing.		✓		
4	understand the meaning of "嗎" and mark its position in a sentence.	✓			
5	read phrases or sentences which have two third tones occurring together.				✓
6	write "你", "我", "他", "大", and "好".			✓	

謝謝你！
Thank You!

你好嗎？

我很好，謝謝！
xiè xie

My Goals

1 Express gratitude and know how to respond when someone says "Thank you"
2 Extend and respond to an apology
3 Know when to use " 不 " (no) and what it represents
4 Know that Chinese characters are made up of different components
5 Become familiar with vocabulary associated with showing gratitude and expressing apologies

New Words

謝謝 thank you 不客氣 you're welcome

New Words

對不起 sorry
duì bù qǐ

沒關係 it's fine
méi guān xi

TIP

Can you differentiate between "沒關係" and "不客氣"?

➤ When someone tells you "對不起", you can say "沒關係" to indicate your acceptance of their apology.

➤ When someone thanks you by saying "謝謝", you can respond humbly by saying "不客氣".

xiè xie · · · xiè xie
謝 謝 你 ！謝 謝 他 ！

qǐng · · · xiè xie tā
請 大 家 謝 謝 她 。

bú yòng xiè · · · bú kè qi
不 用 謝 ，不 客 氣 ！

duì bù qǐ · · · méi guān xi
對 不 起 ！沒 關 係 ！

New Words

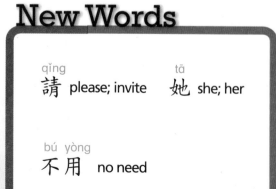

qǐng · · · · · · tā
請 please; invite　她 she; her

bú yòng
不 用　no need

Let's Learn GRAMMAR

xiè　xie
謝謝

xiè　xie
謝謝你！

xiè　xie
謝謝他！

xiè　xie
謝謝你們！

xiè　xie
謝謝他們！

xiè　xie
謝謝大家！

bú　kè　qì
不客氣

bú　kè　qì
不客氣！

bú　yòng　kè　qì
不用客氣！

qǐng　bú　yòng　kè　qì
請不用客氣！

TIP

"不客氣" and "不用客氣" have the same meaning; they are used to respond to an expression of gratitude.

TIP

"謝謝" is a common phrase used in conversations.

➤ If the person whom we wish to thank is in front of us, we can simply say "謝謝".

➤ When using pronouns such as "他", "你們", and "大家", "謝謝" should precede the pronouns.

Julie 好嗎 ？

bù
不

tā
她很好 。

tā bù
她不好 。

好　　不好 (bù)

duì　　bú duì
對　　不對

"不對" means "incorrect"; "對" means "right" or "correct".

yòng　　bú yòng
用　　不用

"不用" means "no need", but "用" means "use".

kè qì　　bú kè qì
客氣　　不客氣

"不客氣" means "you're welcome", but "客氣" means "polite".

xiè xie　　bú yòng xiè
謝謝　　不用謝

Go 100

WANT TO LEARN MORE?

Check out the Text > Sentence Pattern section in the Go100 CD.

True or False?

Circle the correct answer.

1 We should talk politely to friends. 對 / 不對

2 When you are sick and people ask you "你好嗎？", you should reply "我很好". 對 / 不對

3 When people help us out, we should say "不用謝" to them. 對 / 不對

4 When people say "謝謝" to us, we should reply "不客氣". 對 / 不對

Structure of Chinese Characters

Some Chinese characters are composed of two parts written side by side. The left and right components may or may not be in proportion to each other, so study each character carefully before you write them.

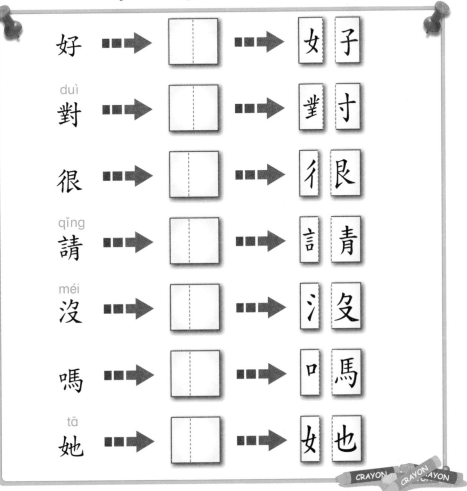

Write out the left and right components of each of the characters below.

① 她 (tā) = ☐ + ☐   ② 們 = ☐ + ☐

③ 好 = ☐ + ☐   ④ 他 = ☐ + ☐

⑤ 你 = ☐ + ☐

TIP Sometimes, the meaning of a Chinese character may be related to its radical component. Do you know what does "女" or "亻" represent when they appear in a character?

女 → 女 → 女

亻 → 人 → 亻

謝謝你！   35

Find a partner and practice the dialogues below.

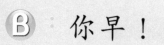 **Task 1**

Ⓐ 你好嗎？

Ⓑ 我很好，<ruby>謝謝<rt>xiè xie</rt></ruby>！

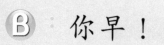 **Task 2**

Ⓐ 你早！

Ⓑ 你早！

Ⓐ 你好嗎？

Ⓑ 我很好，<ruby>謝謝<rt>xiè xie</rt></ruby>你！

Ⓐ <ruby>請不用客氣<rt>qǐng bú yòng kè qì</rt></ruby>。

⭐ Task 3

Ⓐ ： 你好！

Ⓑ ： 你好！

Ⓐ ： Tom 他好嗎？

Ⓑ ： Tom 很好。<ruby>謝謝<rt>xiè xie</rt></ruby>！

Ⓐ ： <ruby>不客氣<rt>bú kè qì</rt></ruby>。

⭐ Task 5

Ⓐ ： <ruby>對不起<rt>duì bù qǐ</rt></ruby>！

Ⓑ ： <ruby>沒關係<rt>méi guān xi</rt></ruby>。

⭐ Task 4

Ⓐ ： Julie 好嗎？

Ⓑ ： <ruby>她<rt>tā</rt></ruby>很好，<ruby>謝謝<rt>xiè xie</rt></ruby>你！

Ⓐ ： <ruby>不用謝<rt>bú yòng xiè</rt></ruby>！

WANT TO LEARN MORE?

Check out the Text > Dialogue section in the Go100 CD.

Let's DO IT

1 How do you show your gratitude or express your apologies in the following situation? Working in pairs, role-play the scenario.

Scenario You accidentally bumped into your classmate along the corridor, causing him to drop the books he was carrying. You helped him pick up the books.

2 Sing a song.

| 1 1 5 5 | 6 6 5 - | 4 4 3 3 | 2 2 1 - |

shuō　　shuō duì bù qǐ　　　shuō　　　shuō méi guān xi

我說*我說對不起，你說你說沒關係。

| 5 5 4 4 | 3 3 2 - | 5 5 4 4 | 3 3 2 - |

shuō　　shuō xiè xie　　　shuō　　　shuō bú kè qì

你說你說謝謝你，我說我說不客氣。

| 1 1 5 5 | 6 6 5 - | 4 4 3 3 | 2 2 1 - |

dōu shì　　péng yǒu　　　dōu shì　　péng yǒu

大家都是*好朋友，大家都是好朋友。

* 說 say
* 都是 all; both

LEARNING LOG

I can...	Excellent	Good	Fair	Needs Improvement
1 understand the meaning of "謝謝" and "對不起" and use them appropriately.				✓
2 reply "不客氣" or "不用客氣" when someone says "謝謝" to me.			✓	
3 reply "沒關係" when someone tells me "對不起".		✓		
4 understand that placing "不" before adjectives may create a negative form.	✓			
5 identify those Chinese characters that are composed of two parts written side by side, from the new words that I have learnt.				✓
6 write "請", "不", "用", "對", and "沒".	✓			

LESSON 4

姓什麼？
What Is Your Last Name?

qǐng wèn　　guì xìng
請問你貴姓？

xìng
我姓謝。

My Goals

1 Introduce myself as well as another person
2 Ask for someone's name politely
3 Understand the sequence of Chinese names
4 Become familiar with vocabulary associated with introducing myself and others

Let's READ

qǐng wèn　　guì xìng
請問你貴姓？

xìng
我姓關。

TIP These are some common Chinese last names. Do you know anyone with any of these last names?

lǐ	wáng	zhāng	liú
李	王	張	劉
chén	yáng	zhào	huáng
陳	楊	趙	黃
xú	zhōu	wú	lín
徐	周	吳	林

qǐng wèn　　xìng shén me
請問她姓什麼？

xìng wáng
她姓王。

New Words

qǐng wèn
請問 may I ask

xìng
姓 last name

guì xìng
貴姓 last name (formal)

shén me
什麼 what

wáng
王 (a Chinese last name)

qǐng wèn　　jiào shén me míng zi
請問他叫什麼名字？

jiào wáng xiǎo guì
他叫王小貴。

jiào　xiǎo míng
我叫小明，
qǐng wèn　　jiào shén me míng zi
請問你叫什麼名字？

jiào
我叫Billy。

New Words

jiào
叫 to call

míng zi
名字 name;
first name

xiǎo guì
小貴 (a Chinese name)

xiǎo míng
小明 (a Chinese name)

qǐng wèn　　guì xìng
你好，請問你貴姓？

de míng zi jiào shén me
你的名字叫什麼？

xìng　　jiào xiǎo míng
我姓謝，叫小明。

dōu jiào　　xiǎo míng
大家都叫我小明。

New Words

dōu
都 all; already

de
的 (particle before a noun)

Let's Learn GRAMMAR

xìng míng
姓 名

míng zi
名 字

xìng   míng
姓   名

"姓名" means "full name". In Chinese, the last name is followed by the first name.

xiǎo míng
謝   小 明

wáng
王   大 關

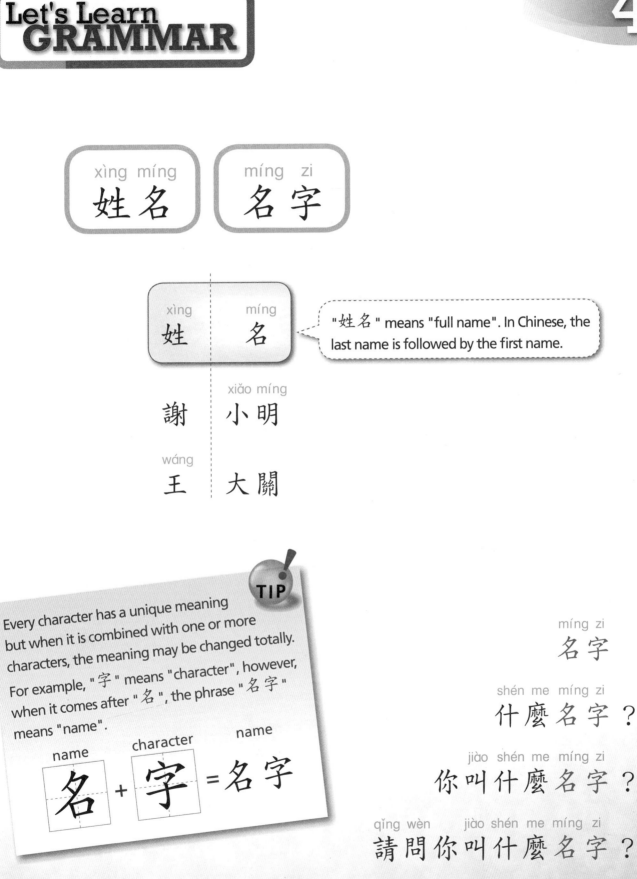

TIP

Every character has a unique meaning but when it is combined with one or more characters, the meaning may be changed totally. For example, "字" means "character", however, when it comes after "名", the phrase "名字" means "name".

name   character   name
名   +   字   =   名字

míng zi
名 字

shén me míng zi
什 麼 名 字 ?

jiào shén me míng zi
你 叫 什 麼 名 字 ?

qǐng wèn   jiào shén me míng zi
請 問 你 叫 什 麼 名 字 ?

de

的

Practice It

Listen to the teacher carefully and follow the instructions.

① 我的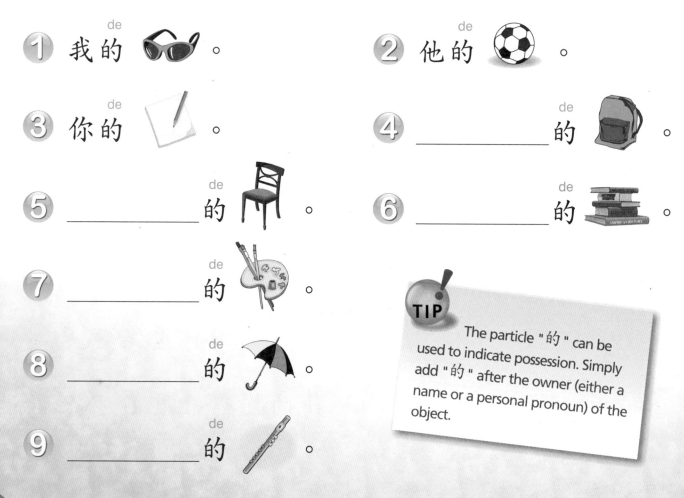

② 他的

③ 你的

④ _____ 的

⑤ _____ 的

⑥ _____ 的

⑦ _____ 的

⑧ _____ 的

⑨ _____ 的

TIP

The particle "的" can be used to indicate possession. Simply add "的" after the owner (either a name or a personal pronoun) of the object.

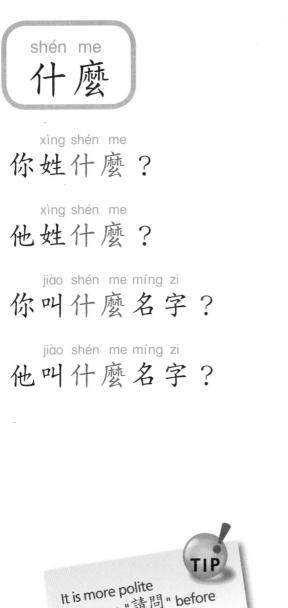

shén me
什麼

xìng shén me
你姓什麼？

xìng shén me
他姓什麼？

jiào shén me míng zi
你叫什麼名字？

jiào shén me míng zi
他叫什麼名字？

TIP
"姓什麼" and "叫什麼" are both used for asking someone's name.
➤ "姓什麼" → asking for last name of the person
➤ "叫什麼" → asking for first name **or** full name of the person

qǐng wèn
請問

qǐng wèn   guì xìng
請問你貴姓？

qǐng wèn   jiào shén me míng zi
請問你叫什麼名字？

qǐng wèn   jiào shén me míng zi
請問他叫什麼名字？

TIP
It is more polite if you use "請問" before asking questions.

Go 100

WANT TO LEARN MORE?

Check out the Text > Sentence Pattern section in the Go100 CD.

Find partner(s) to practice the dialogues below.

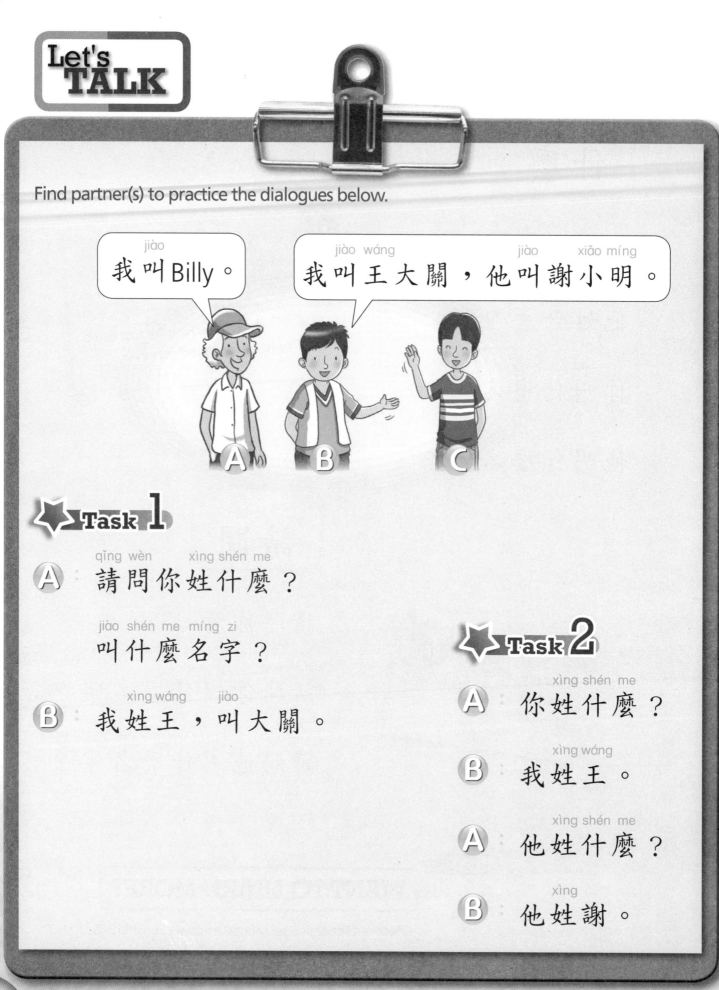

我叫Billy。

我叫王大關，他叫謝小明。

★ Task 1

Ⓐ 請問你姓什麼？
叫什麼名字？

Ⓑ 我姓王，叫大關。

★ Task 2

Ⓐ 你姓什麼？

Ⓑ 我姓王。

Ⓐ 他姓什麼？

Ⓑ 他姓謝。

★ Task 3

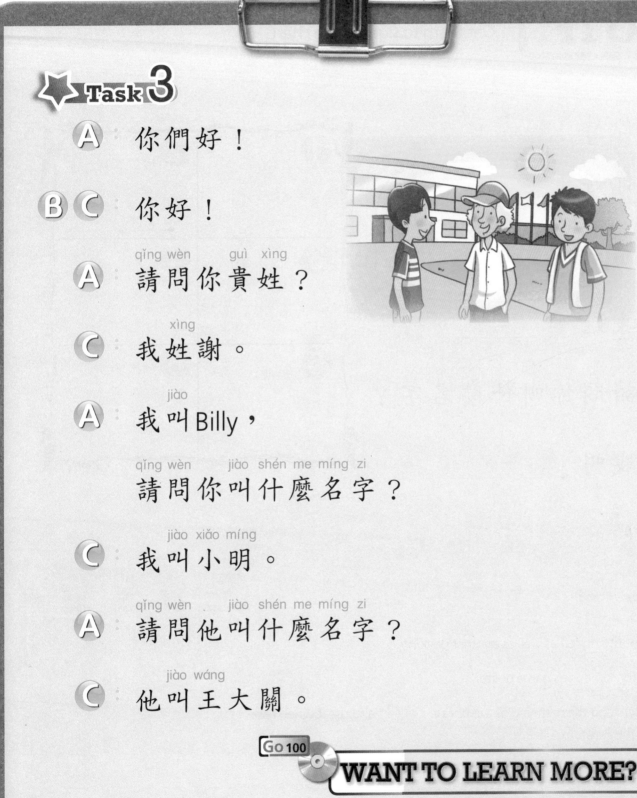

A: 你們好！

B C: 你好！

　　qǐng wèn　　guì xìng
A: 請問你貴姓？

　　xìng
C: 我姓謝。

　　jiào
A: 我叫Billy，

　　qǐng wèn　　jiào shén me míng zi
　　請問你叫什麼名字？

　　jiào xiǎo míng
C: 我叫小明。

　　qǐng wèn　　jiào shén me míng zi
A: 請問他叫什麼名字？

　　jiào wáng
C: 他叫王大關。

Go 100

WANT TO LEARN MORE?

Check out the Text > Dialogue section in the Go100 CD.

Find partners and practice the dialogue below.
Get them to sign on the chart.

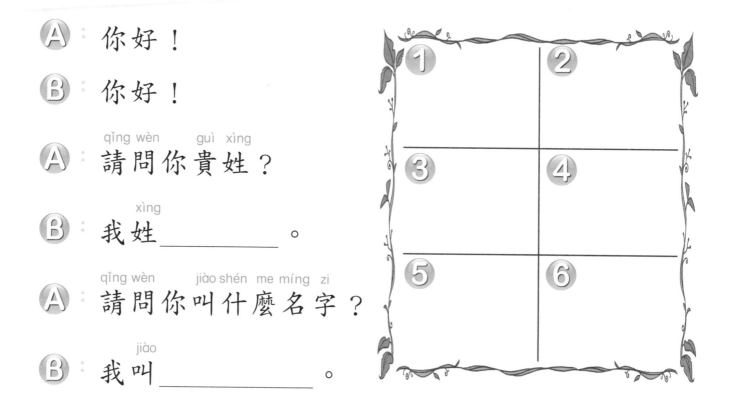

Ⓐ : 你好！

Ⓑ : 你好！

　　　qǐng wèn　　guì xìng
Ⓐ : 請問你貴姓？

　　　　　xìng
Ⓑ : 我姓＿＿＿＿＿。

　　　qǐng wèn　　jiào shén me míng zi
Ⓐ : 請問你叫什麼名字？

　　　　　jiào
Ⓑ : 我叫＿＿＿＿＿＿。

LEARNING LOG

I can...

		Excellent	Good	Fair	Needs Improvement
1	introduce myself as well as another person.	✓			
2	ask for someone's name politely.		✓	✓	
3	understand the meaning of the phrase "請問" and use it when I ask questions.			✓	
4	use the particle "的" to indicate possession.				✓
5	understand the sequence of Chinese names.	✓			
6	write "問", "的", "叫", "名", and "字".		✓		

星期幾？
What Day Is
Today?

2009 年 9 月
(nián) (yuè)

星期日 xīng qí rì	星期一 xīng qí yī	星期二 xīng qí èr	星期三 xīng qí sān	星期四 xīng qí sì	星期五 xīng qí wǔ	星期六 xīng qí liù
		1 Dad's	2	3	4	5
6	7	8 School	9 camp	10	11	12
13	14	15	16	17	18 Swimming	19
20 Ian's	21	22	23	24	Class 5p.m. 25	26
27	28	29	30			

My Goals

1　Learn how to ask or say the date

2　Ask or answer questions relating to quantities and number of days

3　Know the origin of Chinese characters and how they are formed

4　Become familiar with vocabulary associated with talking about dates

xīng qí
星期

xīng qí yǒu tiān
一個星期有七天。

| xīng qí yī 星期一 | xīng qí èr 星期二 | xīng qí sān 星期三 |
| Monday | Tuesday | Wednesday |

| xīng qí sì 星期四 | xīng qí wǔ 星期五 | xīng qí liù 星期六 |
| Thursday | Friday | Saturday |

xīng qí rì 星期日
Sunday

TIP

When people say "星期天", they mean Sunday; both "星期天" and "星期日" refer to Sunday.

New Words

| xīng qí 星期 week | yǒu 有 have |
| tiān 天 day; sky | rì 日 day; date |

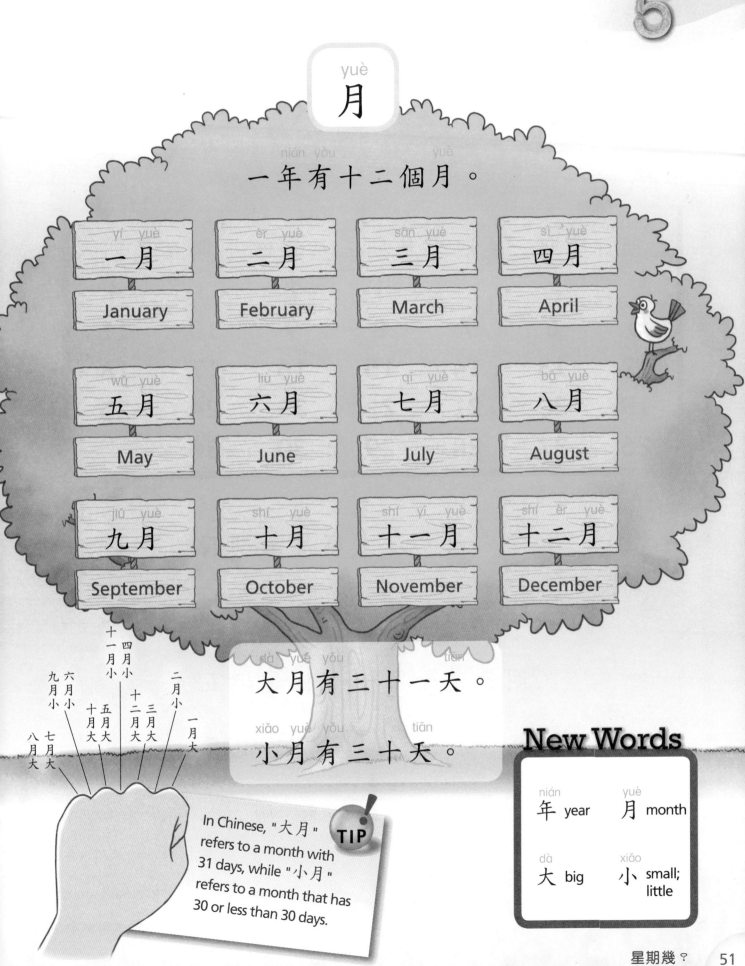

yuè
月

nián yǒu yuè
一年有十二個月。

yī yuè 一月	èr yuè 二月	sān yuè 三月	sì yuè 四月
January	February	March	April

wǔ yuè 五月	liù yuè 六月	qī yuè 七月	bā yuè 八月
May	June	July	August

jiǔ yuè 九月	shí yuè 十月	shí yī yuè 十一月	shí èr yuè 十二月
September	October	November	December

十一月小　四月小
九月小　六月小
　　　十二月大　五月大　十月大
　　　三月大　二月小
　　　　　一月大
八月大　七月大

dà yuè yǒu tiān
大月有三十一天。

xiǎo yuè yǒu tiān
小月有三十天。

TIP

In Chinese, "大月" refers to a month with 31 days, while "小月" refers to a month that has 30 or less than 30 days.

New Words

nián 年 year	yuè 月 month
dà 大 big	xiǎo 小 small; little

jīn tiān　　zuó tiān　　míng tiān
今天 / 昨天 / 明天

nián　qī yuè
二〇〇九年 七月

xīng qí rì 星期日	xīng qí yī 星期一	xīng qí èr 星期二	xīng qí sān 星期三	xīng qí sì 星期四	xīng qí wǔ 星期五	xīng qí liù 星期六
			1	2	3	4
5	6	7	8	9	10	11
12	13	14	15	16	17	18
19	20	21	22	23	24	25
26	27	28	29	30	31	

今天

jīn tiān shì　qī yuè　　　　rì xīng qí sì
今天是七月十六日星期四。

zuó tiān shì　qī yuè　　　　rì xīng qí sān
昨天是七月十五日星期三。

míng tiān shì　qī yuè　　　　rì xīng qí wǔ
明天是七月十七日星期五。

New Words

jīn tiān 今天 today	zuó tiān 昨天 yesterday
míng tiān 明天 tomorrow	shì 是 to be (am, are, is)

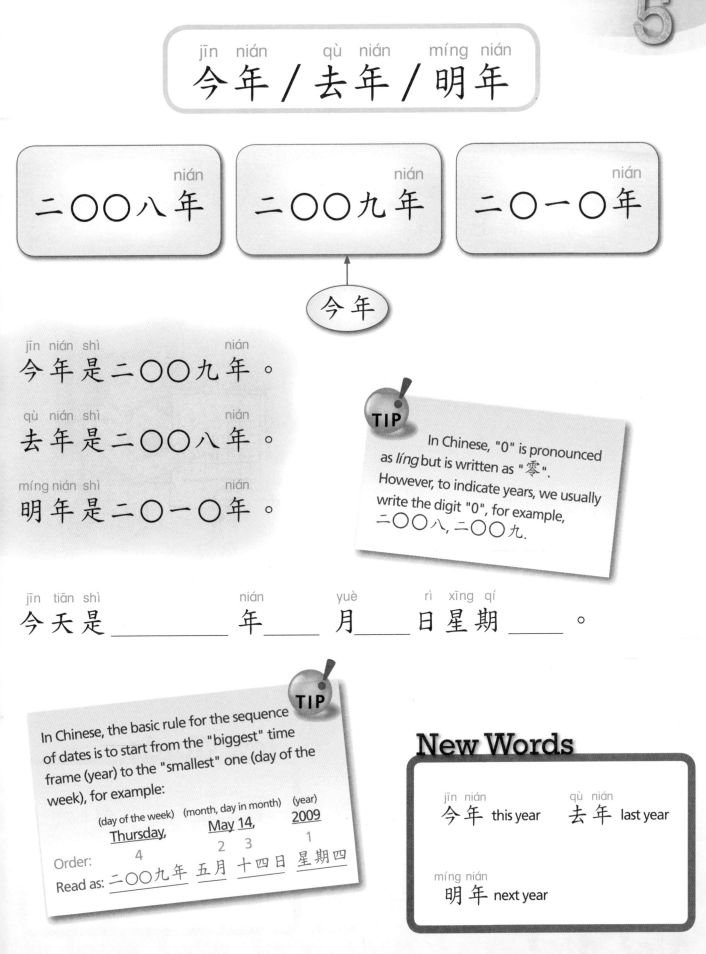

jīn nián / qù nián / míng nián
今年 / 去年 / 明年

二〇〇八年 (nián)   二〇〇九年 (nián)   二〇一〇年 (nián)

今年

jīn nián shì ... nián
今年是二〇〇九年。

qù nián shì ... nián
去年是二〇〇八年。

míng nián shì ... nián
明年是二〇一〇年。

TIP
In Chinese, "0" is pronounced as *líng* but is written as "零". However, to indicate years, we usually write the digit "0", for example, 二〇〇八, 二〇〇九.

jīn tiān shì ... nián ... yuè ... rì xīng qí
今天是_____年___月___日星期___。

TIP
In Chinese, the basic rule for the sequence of dates is to start from the "biggest" time frame (year) to the "smallest" one (day of the week), for example:

(day of the week) Thursday,	(month, day in month) May 14,	(year) 2009
Order: 4	2 3	1
Read as: 星期四	十四日 五月	二〇〇九年

New Words

jīn nián
今年 this year

qù nián
去年 last year

míng nián
明年 next year

xīng qí　　yǒu　　tiān
一星期，有七天，

xīng qí　yī　dào xīng qí　rì
星期一到星期日，

sì　yuè　　rì xīng qí　jǐ
四月一日星期幾？

zhè ge yuè yǒu jǐ　xīng qí
這個月有幾星期？

New Words

dào 到 to arrive		zhè ge 這個 this
jǐ 幾 which; how many; a few		

Let's Learn GRAMMAR

yǒu
有

xīng qí yǒu tiān
一個星期有七天，

sān yuè yǒu tiān
三月有三十一天。

zhè ge yuè yǒu tiān
這個月有三十天。

nián yǒu tiān
一年有三百六十五天。

yǒu bēi zi
我有杯子(cup)。

yǒu shū
Tom 有書(book)。

dào
到

sì yuè rì dào sì yuè rì yǒu tiān
四月一日到四月二十日有二十天。

qī yuè rì dào bā yuè rì yǒu tiān
七月一日到八月三十一日有六十二天。

沒有
méi yǒu

èr yuè méi yǒu　　　rì
二月沒有三十日。

liù yuè méi yǒu　　　　rì
六月沒有三十一日。

méi yǒu jiě jie
他沒有姊姊(sister)。

méi yǒu bēi bāo
我沒有背包(backpack)。

這個
zhè ge

zhè ge yuè yǒu jǐ tiān
這個月有幾天？

zhè ge yuè yǒu　　　　　tiān
這個月有三十一天。

zhè ge yuè yǒu jǐ ge xīng qí
這個月有幾個星期？

期

zhè ge zì　　　　　shì　　　zì
這個字(character)是什麼字？

WANT TO LEARN MORE?

Check out the Text > Sentence Pattern section in the Go100 CD.

⭐ Structure of Chinese Characters

Some Chinese characters are composed of two parts written top to bottom. The top and bottom components may or may not be in proportion to each other, so study each character carefully before you write them.

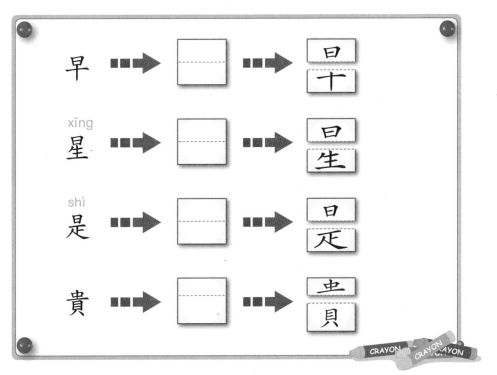

⭐ The Origin of Chinese Characters

Many Chinese characters evolved from illustrations. Below are some examples. Can you tell what the illustrations mean? Write the English meaning in the brackets.

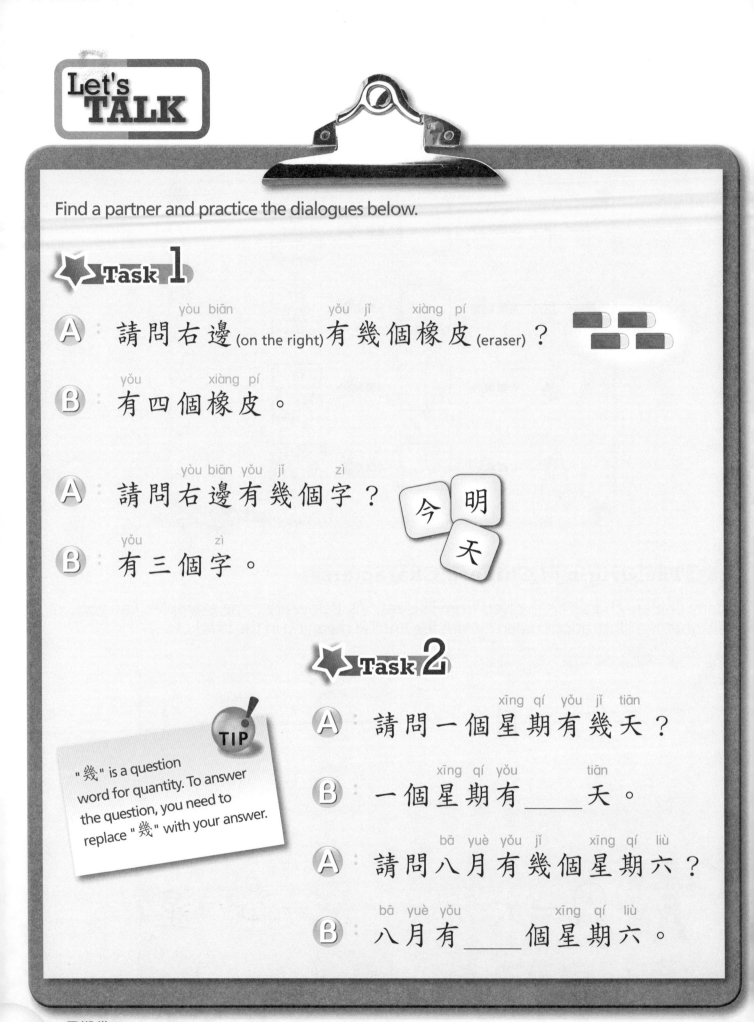

Let's TALK

Find a partner and practice the dialogues below.

⭐Task 1

Ⓐ ： 請問右邊(on the right)有幾個橡皮(eraser)？

Ⓑ ： 有四個橡皮。

Ⓐ ： 請問右邊有幾個字？

Ⓑ ： 有三個字。

今 明 天

⭐Task 2

Ⓐ ： 請問一個星期有幾天？

Ⓑ ： 一個星期有＿＿天。

Ⓐ ： 請問八月有幾個星期六？

Ⓑ ： 八月有＿＿個星期六。

TIP

"幾" is a question word for quantity. To answer the question, you need to replace "幾" with your answer.

A ： 請問昨天是星期幾？
　　zuó tiān shì xīng qí jǐ

B ： 昨天是＿＿＿＿＿＿＿＿。
　　zuó tiān shì

A ： 請問今天是幾月幾日？
　　jīn tiān shì jǐ yuè jǐ rì

B ： 今天是＿＿＿＿＿＿＿。
　　jīn tiān shì

A ： 請問明年是幾年？
　　míng nián shì jǐ nián

B ： 明年是＿＿＿＿＿＿＿。
　　míng nián shì

A ： 請問五月一日到五月五日有幾天？
　　wǔ yuè rì dào wǔ yuè rì yǒu jǐ tiān

B ： 有＿＿＿＿＿＿＿。
　　yǒu

Go 100

WANT TO LEARN MORE?

Check out the Text > Dialogue section in the Go100 CD.

Let's DO IT

^{shēng rì}
"生日" means birthday. Together with five other classmates, practice the dialogue below. Record their birthdays in the table provided.

A : ^{shēng rì shì jǐ nián jǐ yuè jǐ rì}
請 問 你 的 生 日 是 幾 年 幾 月 幾 日 ？

B : ^{shēng rì shì nián yuè rì}
我 的 生 日 是 ＿＿ 年 ＿＿ 月 ＿＿ 日 。

A : ^{jīn nián yuè rì shì xīng qí jǐ}
今 年 的 ＿＿ 月 ＿＿ 日 是 星 期 幾 ？

B : ^{jīn nián yuè rì shì xīng qí}
今 年 的 ＿＿ 月 ＿＿ 日 是 星 期 ＿＿ 。

	Name	Birthday	On which day does the birthday fall on this year?
1			
2			
3			
4			
5			

LEARNING LOG

I can...

		Excellent	Good	Fair	Needs Improvement
1	ask about dates politely.	✓			
2	talk about dates in Chinese, in the order of year, month, and day.		✓		
3	ask and talk about a specific range of days.			✓	
4	identify words that are made up of top and bottom components and know that Chinese characters evolved from illustrations.				✓
5	write "有", "月", "天", "今", and "日".	✓			

幾個人？
How Many People Are There in Your Family?

jiā
家

My Goals

1 Name family members in Chinese
2 Count and introduce my family members to others
3 Ask someone about his/her family
4 Become familiar with vocabulary associated with introducing family members

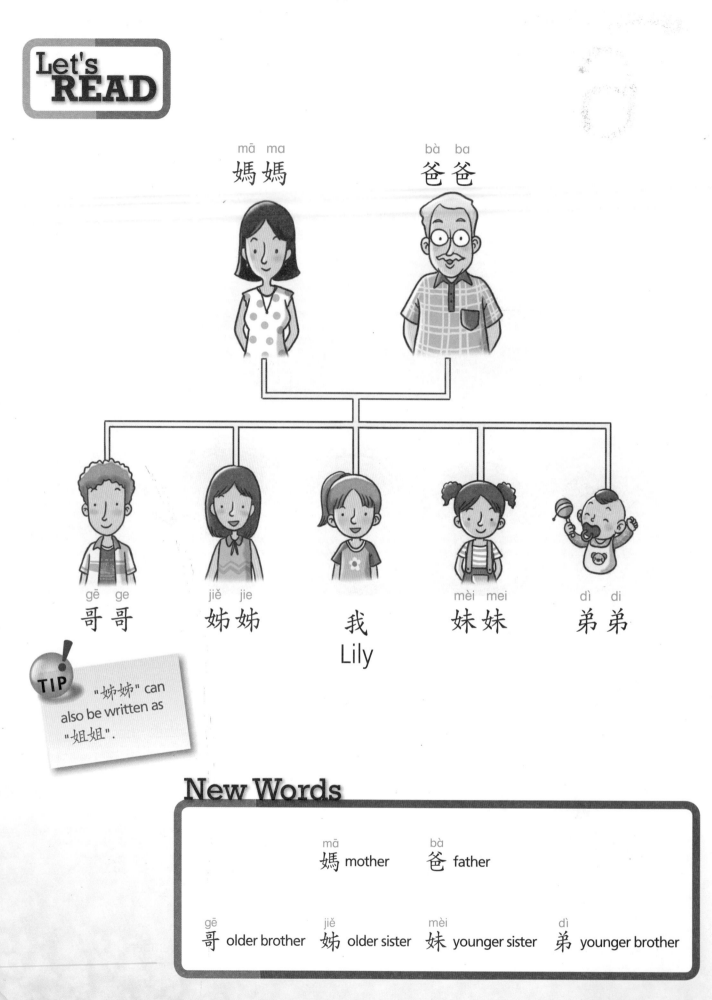

mā ma
媽媽

bà ba
爸爸

gē ge
哥哥

jiě jie
姊姊

我
Lily

mèi mei
妹妹

dì di
弟弟

TIP "姊姊" can also be written as "姐姐".

New Words

mā
媽 mother

bà
爸 father

gē
哥 older brother

jiě
姊 older sister

mèi
妹 younger sister

dì
弟 younger brother

請問你家幾個人？
jiā   rén

爸爸、媽媽、哥哥、姊姊、
bà ba   mā ma   gē ge   jiě jie

弟弟、妹妹、還有我，
dì di   mèi mei   hái yǒu

我家一共七個人。
jiā   yí gòng   rén

請問你家幾口人？
jiā   kǒu rén

TIP

When introducing or inquiring about the number of family members, the measure word "口" used to be the formal usage. But these days, the measure word "個" is also commonly used. For example, some people may ask, "你家有幾個人？"

New Words

家 jiā home; family	口 kǒu (a measure word used for counting family members)	人 rén people; human beings
還有 hái yǒu still; also; and	一共 yí gòng in total	

有 / 沒有

	有	一個	哥哥。 gē ge
我	沒有	哥哥。 gē ge	

我有兩個姊姊。
jiě jie

你有一個妹妹。
mèi mei

我沒有哥哥。
gē ge

他沒有妹妹。
mèi mei

他有姊姊。
jiě jie

我沒有妹妹。
mèi mei

TIP

"沒有" is usually not used together with measure words, so you will never hear people say "我沒有兩個哥哥" in Chinese.

有⋯⋯嗎？／有沒有？

你	有	mèi mei 妹妹	嗎？
	有沒有	mèi mei 妹妹？	

mèi mei
你有妹妹嗎？

mèi mei
你有沒有妹妹？

jiě jie
他有姊姊嗎？

jiě jie
他有沒有姊姊？

TIP
"有⋯⋯嗎？" and "有沒有？" have the same meaning; they are sentence patterns that indicate a query.

一月有三十一日嗎？

一月有沒有三十一日？

有……，還有……

我	有	哥哥 (gē ge)，	還有 (hái yǒu)	弟弟 (dì di)。

我有姊姊 (jiě jie)，還有妹妹 (hái yǒu mèi mei)。

我有筆 (bǐ) (pen)，還有書 (hái yǒu shū) (book)。

他有一個哥哥 (gē ge)、兩個姊姊 (jiě jie)，還有三個妹妹 (hái yǒu mèi mei)。

一共 (yí gòng)

他家一共七個人 (jiā yí gòng rén)。

我家一共九口人 (jiā yí gòng kǒu rén)。

七月、八月一共六十二天 (yí gòng)。

 WANT TO LEARN MORE?

Check out the Text > Sentence Pattern section in the Go100 CD.

 **Read and Write**

Look at the pictures. Then fill in the blanks with the appropriate words.

① 我家有＿＿七＿＿口人，
（jiā）　　　（kǒu rén）

　我有＿＿二＿＿個弟弟，
　　　（dì di）

　還有＿＿一＿＿個妹妹。
　（hái yǒu）　　　（mèi mei）

② 我有爸爸、~~媽媽~~，
　　（bà ba）

　還有一個＿哥哥＿。
　（hái yǒu）

　我家一共＿＿四＿＿口人。
　（jiā yí gòng）　　　（kǒu rén）

③ 我有＿＿○＿＿弟弟，
　　　（dì di）

　＿＿二＿＿哥哥。
　　（gē ge）

　我＿＿○＿＿姊姊，＿＿○＿＿妹妹。
　　（jiě jie）　　　（mèi mei）

Task 1

Find a partner and practice the dialogue below.

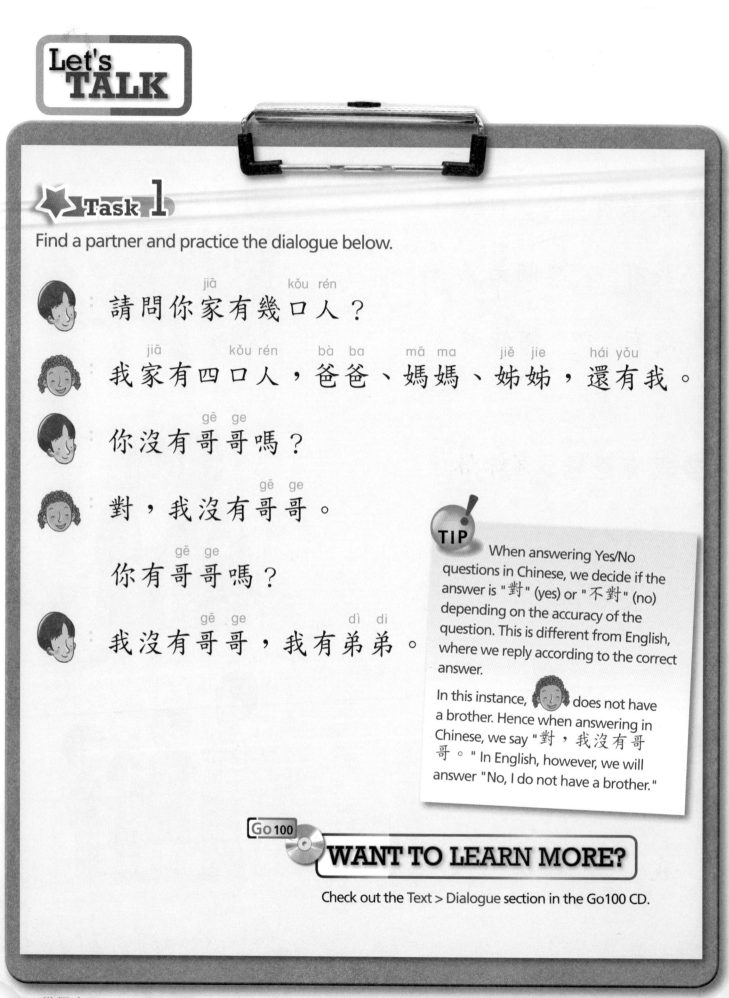

請問你家有幾口人？
jiā　　kǒu rén

我家有四口人，爸爸、媽媽、姊姊，還有我。
jiā　　kǒu rén　　bà ba　　mā ma　　jiě jie　　hái yǒu

你沒有哥哥嗎？
gē ge

對，我沒有哥哥。
gē ge

你有哥哥嗎？
gē ge

我沒有哥哥，我有弟弟。
gē ge　　dì di

TIP

When answering Yes/No questions in Chinese, we decide if the answer is "對" (yes) or "不對" (no) depending on the accuracy of the question. This is different from English, where we reply according to the correct answer.

In this instance, does not have a brother. Hence when answering in Chinese, we say "對，我沒有哥哥。" In English, however, we will answer "No, I do not have a brother."

Go 100

WANT TO LEARN MORE?

Check out the Text > Dialogue section in the Go100 CD.

Task 2

Find a partner and practice the dialogue. Imagine you are and answer the questions in Chinese.

請問你家有幾口人？

我家有＿＿＿＿＿＿。

你有沒有妹妹？

＿＿＿＿＿＿＿＿。

請問你有弟弟嗎？

＿＿＿＿＿＿＿＿。

你弟弟叫什麼名字？

他叫王小星。

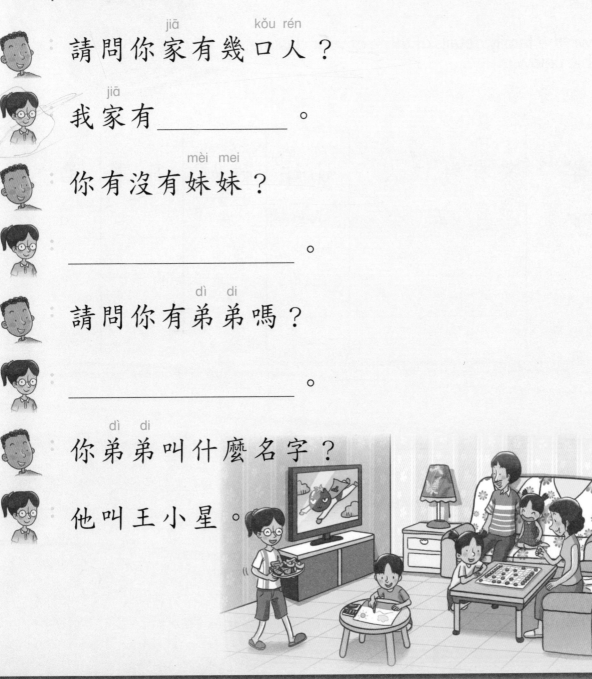

Bring a family photograph or picture to school.

Bring a family photograph or picture to school. Show it to the class and introduce your family members. You must include the following information in your presentation: the number of people in your family, who they are, and their names.

Write down the family details of three of your classmates in the table below.

名字	jiā kǒu rén 家有幾口人？	jiě jie 姊姊	mèi mei 妹妹	gē ge 哥哥	dì di 弟弟
e.g. Adam	五	Ada	-	-	Jack
1					
2					
3					

多少錢？
How Much Is This?

Cashier

Monthly Special

$12.50 $2<del>0</del> $21.50

$4 $5 $13

My Goals

1 Understand conversations related to buying and selling things
2 Ask questions related to the quantity or price of a product
3 Clearly identify the product I wish to buy
4 Become familiar with vocabulary associated with buying things

New Words

yào 要 need; want	mǎi 買 buy	duō shǎo 多少 how many; how much
qián 錢 money	kuài 塊 (unit of currency)	

Let's CHANT Go 100

請問那個多少錢？
nà ge duō shǎo qián

太貴了，不要買！
tài guì le　　　mǎi

便宜一點兒好不好？
pián yí yì diǎnr

算算一共多少錢？
suàn suàn　　　duō shǎo qián

便宜一點兒好不好？
pián yí yì diǎnr

TIP
Do you notice the difference in the pinyin for "一點兒"?
"一點兒" has a special pronunciation; "兒" is no longer an independent syllable when attached with "點". Hence when we pronounce "一點兒", we have to raise the tip of our tongue and curl back over the tongue itself when saying the word "點".

New Words

那個 that (nà ge)	貴 expensive (guì)	太貴了 too expensive (tài guì le)
便宜 cheap (pián yí)	一點兒 a little bit (yì diǎnr)	算 to calculate or count (suàn)

這個 / 那個 _{nà ge}

這個九塊錢，
kuài qián

那個十塊錢，
nà ge　kuài qián

一共十九塊錢。
kuài qián

那個
nà ge

這個

請問這個多少錢？
duō shǎo qián

請問那個多少錢？
nà ge　duō shǎo qián

我要買蘋果(apple)，
yào mǎi píng guǒ

5塊
kuài

請問蘋果多少錢？
píng guǒ　duō shǎo qián

便宜 / 貴
pián yí / guì

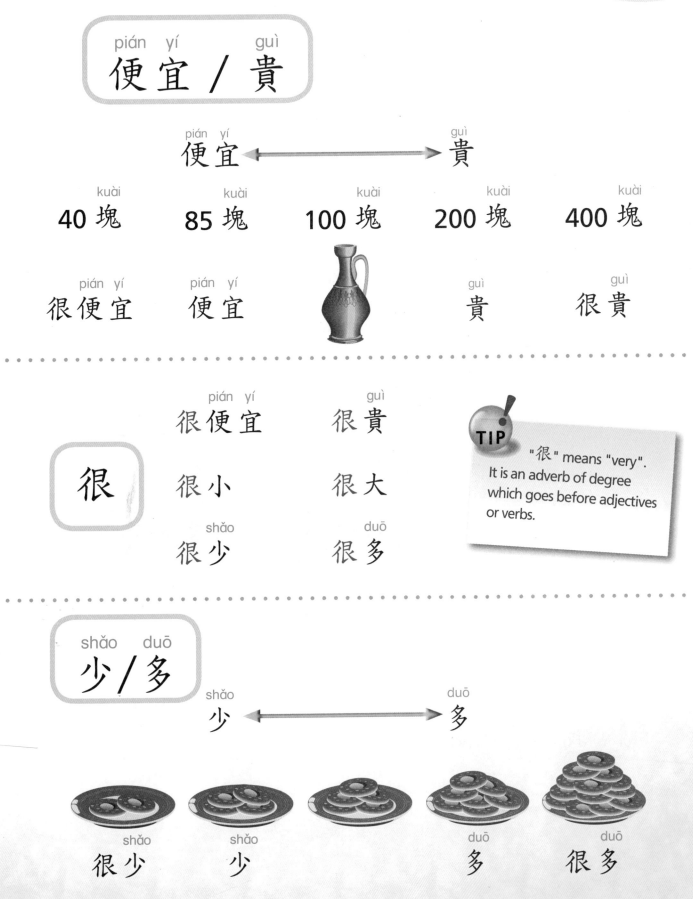

pián yí 便宜 ⟷ guì 貴

kuài	kuài	kuài	kuài	kuài
40 塊	85 塊	100 塊	200 塊	400 塊

pián yí 很便宜　pián yí 便宜　　　　guì 貴　guì 很貴

很

很便宜 pián yí　很貴 guì

很小　很大

很少 shǎo　很多 duō

TIP

"很" means "very". It is an adverb of degree which goes before adjectives or verbs.

少 / 多
shǎo duō

少 shǎo ⟷ 多 duō

很少 shǎo　少 shǎo　　　多 duō　很多 duō

要 / 要……嗎？

（yào / yào）

Ⓐ：請問你要買什麼？
（yào mǎi）

Ⓑ：我要買五個撲滿 (piggy bank)。
（yào mǎi）（pū mǎn）

Ⓐ：你要買裙子 (skirt) 嗎？
（yào mǎi qún zi）

Ⓑ：我不買裙子，我要買鞋子 (shoes)。
（mǎi qún zi）（yào mǎi xié zi）

Ⓐ：請問你要買這個嗎？
（yào mǎi）

Ⓑ：我不買，謝謝。
（mǎi）

幾 ／ 多少
(duō shǎo)

TIP

When asking questions related to quantity,
➤ "幾" usually applies to numbers below 10.
➤ "多少" applies to any other number.
➤ use "多少" if you are unable to estimate the quantity.

When asking about one's age,
➤ "你幾歲？" is used when we talk to children 10 years old or younger.
➤ "你多大？" is used when we talk to people of the same age. It can also be used when talking to children of any age.
➤ "您多大年紀？" (nín nián jì) is used when we talk to people who are older than us.

你有幾個姊姊？

一個星期有幾天？

你家有幾口人？

(A) 你幾歲？ (suì)

(B) 我八歲。 (suì)

(A) 他幾歲？ (suì)

(B) 他十歲。 (suì)

這個多少錢？ (duō shǎo qián)

那個多少錢？ (nà ge duō shǎo qián)

十月有多少天？ (duō shǎo)

一年有多少天？ (duō shǎo)

New Words

歲 (suì) years of age
(a measure word)

Go100

WANT TO LEARN MORE?

Check out the Text > Sentence Pattern section in the Go100 CD.

Find a partner and practice the dialogues below.

⭐ **Task 1**

Ⓐ : 請問你要買什麼？
yào mǎi

Ⓑ : 我要買這個，請問這個多少錢？
yào mǎi duō shǎo qián

Ⓐ : 這個10塊。
kuài

Ⓑ : 我要買兩個，
yào mǎi

算算一共多少錢？
suàn suàn duō shǎo qián

Ⓐ : 兩個一共20塊。
kuài

⭐ **Want More Practice?**

Replace the red text with the items below:

① 27
kuài
12 塊

②
kuài
6 塊

③
kuài
37 塊

[Go 100]

WANT TO LEARN MORE?

Check out the Text > Dialogue section in the Go100 CD.

⭐ Task 2

Ⓐ： 請問你要買什麼？
<small>yào mǎi</small>

Ⓑ： 我要買這個，請問這個多少錢？
<small>yào mǎi　　　　　　　　　duō shǎo qián</small>

Ⓐ： 這個27塊。
<small>kuài</small>

Ⓑ： 27塊太貴了，便宜一點兒好不好？
<small>kuài tài guì le　　pián yí yì diǎnr</small>

Ⓐ： 你買那個好嗎？
<small>mǎi nà ge</small>

　　 那個13塊，很便宜。
<small>nà ge　　kuài　　　pián yí</small>

Ⓑ： 13塊很便宜，我要買兩個。
<small>kuài　　pián yí　　　yào mǎi</small>

⭐ Want More Practice?

Replace the red text with the items below:

① 39 塊 <small>kuài</small>　　② 8 塊 <small>kuài</small>　　③ 99 塊 <small>kuài</small>　　④ 2 塊 <small>kuài</small>

Work in pairs. One of you will pretend to be a stall owner while the other will act as a customer.

Using the vocabulary and sentence patterns you have just learned, the "stall owner" must find out what the "customer" wants to buy and calculate the total cost of the purchase. The "customer" may try to bargain with the "stall owner" for a better price if he/she feels that the item is too expensive. Write down your transaction details in the table below.

Item	List Price	Quantity	Discounted Price	Subtotal
			Total:	

幾點鐘？
What Time Is It?

My Goals

1 Ask someone for the time
2 Tell time in Chinese
3 Ask or say if a person is at a specific location at a particular time
4 Become familiar with vocabulary associated with telling time

①
diǎn
三 點

②
diǎn
六 點

③
diǎn
八 點

④
diǎn bàn
三 點 半

⑤
diǎn bàn
十 點 半

⑥
diǎn bàn
七 點 半

bàn
" 半 " means half.

Cut a cake into half.

一 個 人 吃(eat)半 個
chī bàn
dàn gāo
蛋糕(cake)。

TIP

1 hour is 60 minutes, half of 60 minutes is 30 minutes.

diǎn fēn diǎn bàn
七 點 三 十 分 = 七 點 半

New Words

diǎn
點 o'clock (indicating time of day)

bàn
半 half

diǎn   fēn
一點三十五分

diǎn   fēn
三點四十分

diǎn   fēn
六點五十分

diǎn   fēn
十二點十分

diǎn   fēn
五點十五分

diǎn   fēn
九點二十五分

New Words

fēn
分 minute

幾點鐘？　83

現在幾點鐘？

現在上午九點鐘。

TIP

When "⋯⋯點鐘" is used to refer to "o' clock", "鐘" can be omitted.

請問現在幾點？

你爸爸今天在家嗎？

現在中午十二點三十五分。

我爸爸今天不在家，
他明天晚上在家。

New Words

在 in	現在 now	⋯⋯點鐘 o'clock (indicating time of day)
上午 morning	中午 noon	晚上 night

Let's CHANT

Go 100

　　　　xiàn zài　　diǎn zhōng
請問現在幾點鐘？

　　xià wǔ　diǎn　　fēn
下午三點五十分，

　　　　fēn　　diǎn zhōng
還有十分四點鐘，

　diǎn bàn shí　　zǒu
四點半時我要走。

New Words

xià wǔ 下午 afternoon	shí 時 time; when
zǒu 走 depart; walk; leave	

zài　　　　zài
在 / 不在

| 他 | ^{zài} 在 | 家。 |
| | ^{zài} 不在 | |

^{zài}
小明在家。

^{zài}
姊姊不在家。

^{zài}
小明的爸爸不在家。

^{zài}
小明的媽媽在家。

xià wǔ　　　diǎn zài
我下午三點在家。

wǎn shàng　　diǎn　　zài
我晚上十點不在家。

TIP　In Chinese, dates and times are generally sequenced "from big to small" (in other words, from general to specific).
For example:

	July	26,	2009
Order:	2 m	3 D	1 y
Read as:	二〇〇九年	七月	二十六日

	9: 14 p.m.	8: 34 a.m.
Order:	2 3 1	2 3 1
Read as:	晚上 9點 14分	上午 8點 34分

在 …… 嗎 ？／ 在 不 在 ？
zài   *zài*   *zài*

| 你 | 在 (*zài*) | 家 | 嗎？ |
| | 在 不 在 (*zài* *zài*) | | ？ |

明天你在家嗎？
zài

明天你在不在家？
zài   *zài*

星期二你在學校(school)嗎？
zài *xué* *xiào*

星期二你在不在學校？
zài   *zài* *xué* *xiào*

星期日下午你哥哥在家嗎？
xià *wǔ*   *zài*

星期日下午你哥哥在不在家？
xià *wǔ*   *zài*   *zài*

Go 100
WANT TO LEARN MORE?

Check out the Text > Sentence Pattern section in the Go100 CD.

Find a partner and practice the dialogues below.

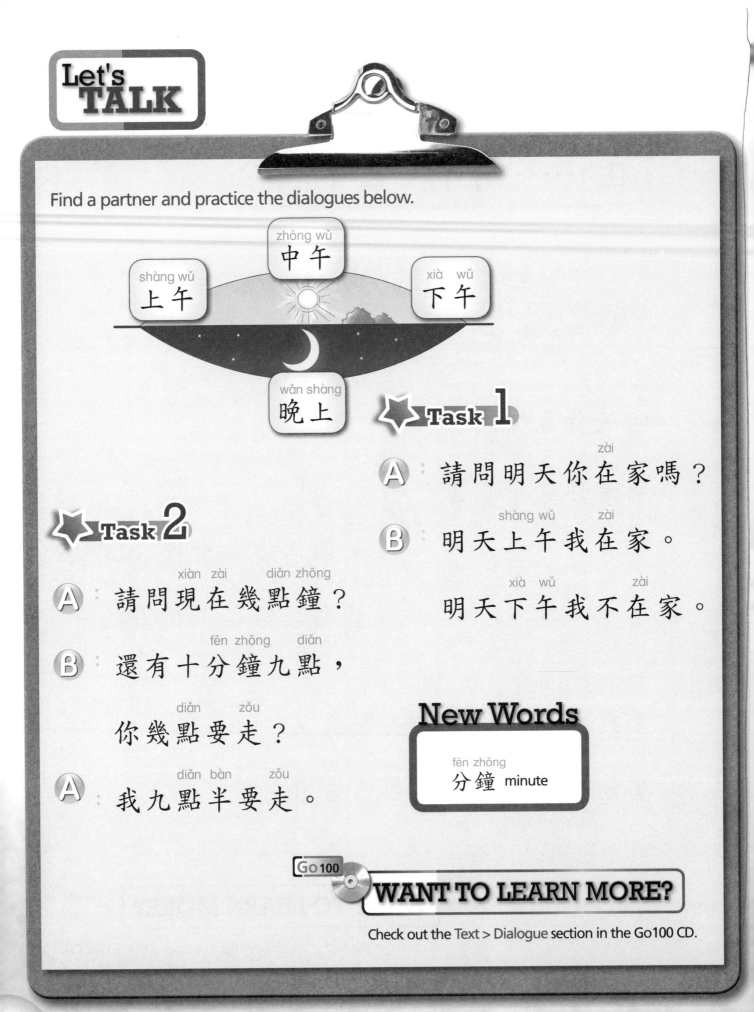

shàng wǔ
上午

zhōng wǔ
中午

xià wǔ
下午

wǎn shàng
晚上

⭐ Task **1**

Ⓐ : 請問明天你在家嗎？
　　　　　　zài

Ⓑ : 明天上午我在家。
　　shàng wǔ　　zài

　　明天下午我不在家。
　　xià wǔ　　　zài

⭐ Task **2**

Ⓐ : 請問現在幾點鐘？
　　　xiàn zài　　diǎn zhōng

Ⓑ : 還有十分鐘九點，
　　　　fēn zhōng　diǎn

　　你幾點要走？
　　　diǎn　　zǒu

Ⓐ : 我九點半要走。
　　diǎn bàn　zǒu

New Words

fēn zhōng
分鐘 minute

Go 100

WANT TO LEARN MORE?

Check out the Text > Dialogue section in the Go100 CD.

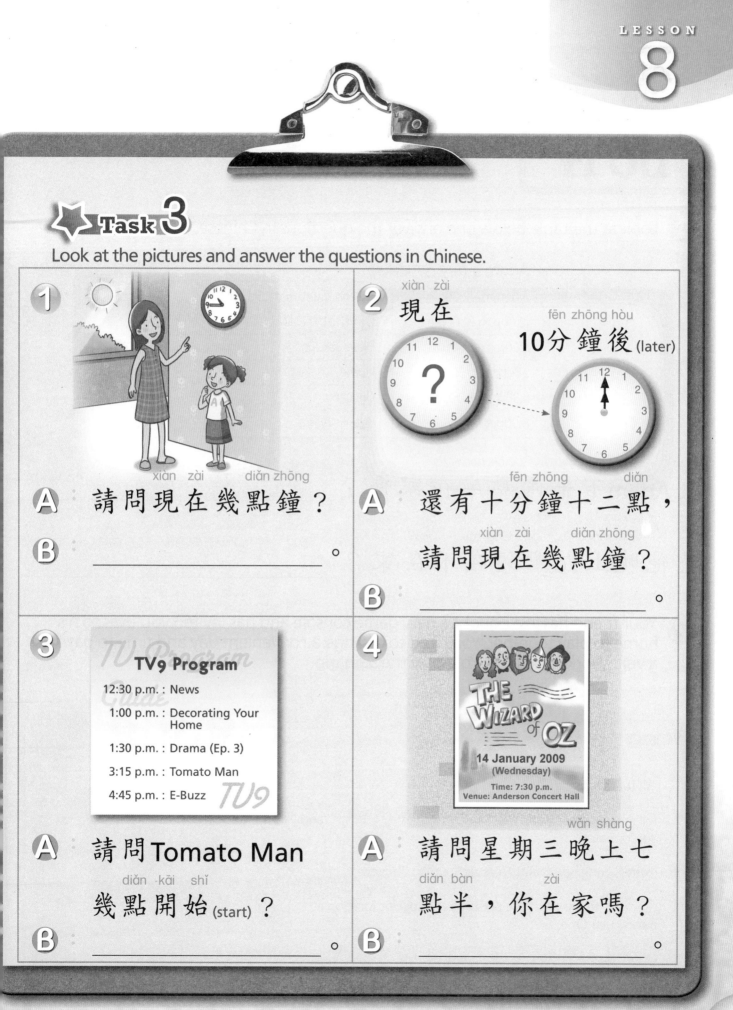

Task 3

Look at the pictures and answer the questions in Chinese.

1

^{xiàn} ^{zài} ^{diǎn} ^{zhōng}
Ⓐ 請問現在幾點鐘？

Ⓑ ＿＿＿＿＿＿＿＿＿＿＿ 。

2

^{xiàn zài}
現在

^{fēn zhōng hòu}
10分鐘後 (later)

^{fēn zhōng} ^{diǎn}
Ⓐ 還有十分鐘十二點，

^{xiàn zài} ^{diǎn zhōng}
請問現在幾點鐘？

Ⓑ ＿＿＿＿＿＿＿＿＿＿＿ 。

3

TV9 Program

12:30 p.m. : News

1:00 p.m. : Decorating Your Home

1:30 p.m. : Drama (Ep. 3)

3:15 p.m. : Tomato Man

4:45 p.m. : E-Buzz

Ⓐ 請問 Tomato Man
^{diǎn} ^{kāi} ^{shǐ}
幾點開始 (start)？

Ⓑ ＿＿＿＿＿＿＿＿＿ 。

4

THE WIZARD of OZ

14 January 2009
(Wednesday)

Time: 7:30 p.m.
Venue: Anderson Concert Hall

^{wǎn shàng}
Ⓐ 請問星期三晚上七
^{diǎn bàn} ^{zài}
點半，你在家嗎？

Ⓑ ＿＿＿＿＿＿＿＿＿ 。

1 Look at the table below and answer the questions in Chinese.

Adam's day schedule	
8:00a.m.-12:00p.m.	Attend classes at school
12:00p.m.-2:00p.m.	Study at the library
2:00p.m.-3:30p.m.	Piano lesson
3:30p.m.-6:30p.m.	Home
6:30p.m.-8:00p.m.	Concert
8:00p.m.	Return home

　　　　　xià　wǔ　　　diǎn bàn　zài
1. Adam下午兩點半在家嗎？＿＿＿＿＿＿＿＿＿＿＿＿＿＿

　　wǎn shàng　　diǎn zhōng zài　　　　zài
2. 他晚上九點鐘在不在家？＿＿＿＿＿＿＿＿＿＿＿＿＿

2 Your friend has just bought a new game console and has invited you over to his home to play together. You need to arrange a convenient day and time to pay him a visit. Working in pairs, role-play the scenario.

LEARNING LOG	I can...	Excellent	Good	Fair	Needs Improvement
	1 ask for the time in Chinese.	✓			
	2 tell time accurately and use "上午", "中午", "下午", and "晚上" appropriately.		✓		
	3 express "one hour" and "half an hour" in Chinese.			✓	
	4 use "在" to ask or say if a person is at a specific location at a particular time.				✓
	5 write "上", "中", "下", "在", and "走".	✓			

LESSON 9

打電話
Making a Phone Call

My Goals

1 Make and answer telephone calls in Chinese
2 Inquire about and tell the telephone number
3 Know the difference between English and Chinese telephone terminology
4 Become familiar with basic vocabulary associated with making and answering telephone calls

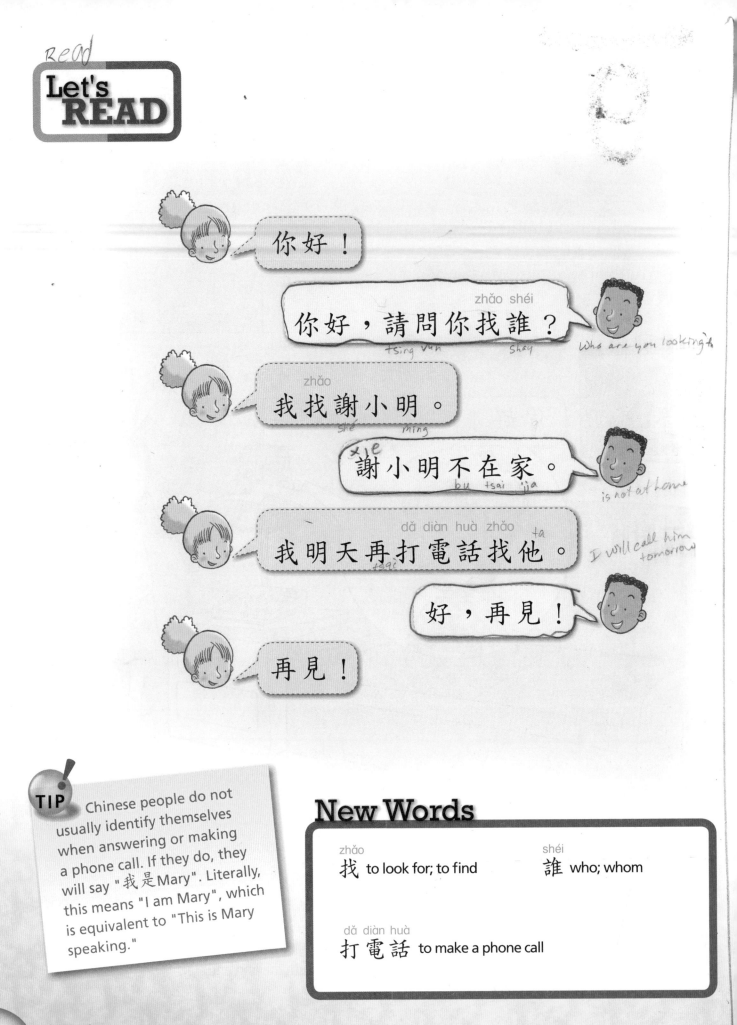

你好！

你好，請問你找誰？
zhǎo shéi
tsing vuh   shay
Who are you looking for

我找謝小明。
zhǎo
shé   ming

謝小明不在家。
xie
bu tsai jia
is not at home

我明天再打電話找他。
dǎ diàn huà zhǎo   ta
tsai
I will call him tomorrow

好，再見！

再見！

TIP Chinese people do not usually identify themselves when answering or making a phone call. If they do, they will say "我是Mary". Literally, this means "I am Mary", which is equivalent to "This is Mary speaking."

New Words

zhǎo 找 to look for; to find	shéi 誰 who; whom

dǎ diàn huà
打電話 to make a phone call

Let's CHANT Go 100

zhǎo nǎ   wèi
請問你找哪一位？

diàn huà   hào
你的電話是幾號？

děng yì děng   lái
等一等，我來了！

shéi dǎ diàn huà zhǎo
是誰打電話找我？

TIP

There are many ways to ask for telephone numbers. "你的電話多少號？" is very commonly used too.

New Words

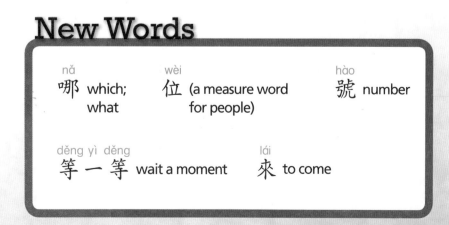

nǎ 哪 which; what	wèi 位 (a measure word for people)	hào 號 number
děng yì děng 等一等 wait a moment	lái 來 to come	

Let's Learn GRAMMAR

shéi
誰

shéi
誰 的 ？

shéi
這 是 誰 的 ？

shéi
這 是 誰 的 家 ？

shéi
誰 ？

zhǎo shéi
你 找 誰 ？

zhǎo shéi
請 問 你 找 誰 ？

shéi zhǎo
誰 找 我 ？

shéi
誰 有 錢 ？

shéi   dǎ diàn huà
誰 在 打 電 話 ？

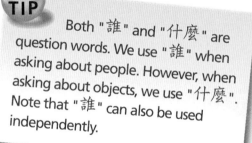

TIP

Both "誰" and "什麼" are question words. We use "誰" when asking about people. However, when asking about objects, we use "什麼". Note that "誰" can also be used independently.

Compare It

① What are the differences between these two characters?

② What are the similarities between these two characters?

zhǎo   wǒ
找   我

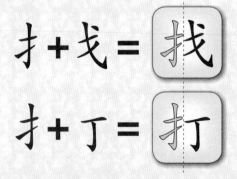

扌 + 戈 = 找

扌 + 丁 = 打

zhǎo

找

zhǎo

哥哥，有人找你。

zhǎo shéi

Ⓐ 請問你找誰？

zhǎo

Ⓑ 我找謝小明。

zhǎo

Ⓐ 你找我哥哥嗎？

zhǎo

Ⓑ 對，我找你哥哥。

Compare It

③ Compare the red components on the left and the right. How are they different?

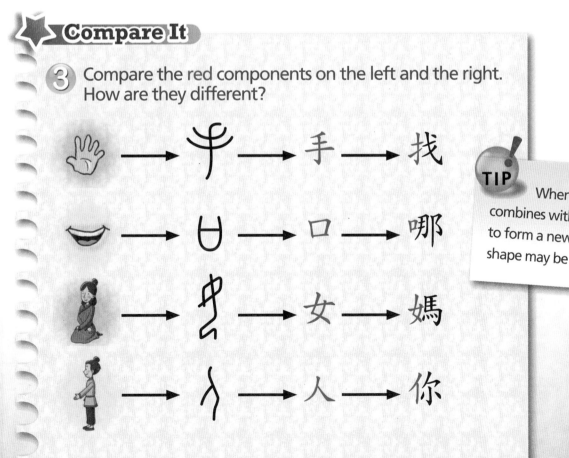

TIP

When a Chinese character combines with another component to form a new word, its form and shape may be modified.

是／不是

他	是	小明的哥哥。
	不是	

你是大關的姊姊。

不是，我不是大關的姊姊。

現在不是三點半，現在是四點半。
明天不是星期一，明天是星期二。

是……嗎？

他	是	謝小明	嗎？

你是小明的弟弟嗎？

今天是星期五嗎？
現在是兩點十五分嗎？

等一下 / 等一等 / 等
děng yí xià   děng yì děng   děng

請你等一下。
děng yí xià

請你等一等。
děng yì děng

請你等十分鐘。
děng

請你再等五分鐘。
děng

我們等你。
děng

TIP

"等一下" and "等一等" are used when you need someone to wait for a short period. They cannot be followed by any mention of a specific time or the person whom one is waiting for. To talk about a specific waiting period or person, we simply use "等".

那 / 哪
nǎ

那位是小明的爸爸。
wèi

哪一位是小明的爸爸？
nǎ   wèi

那個是我的電話。

哪一個是你的電話？
nǎ

TIP

"那" and "哪" have different usages. In this instance, "那(一個)" refers to "that one"; the target or object is certain. It is usually used in declarative sentences. "哪(一個)" has the meaning of "which one" and is usually used in interrogative sentences.

Go 100

WANT TO LEARN MORE?

Check out the Text > Sentence Pattern section in the Go100 CD.

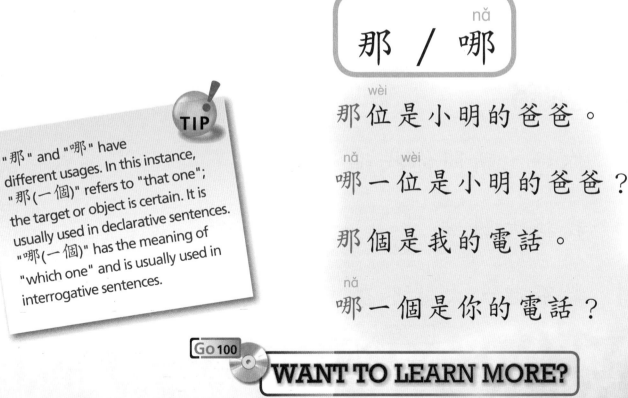

Find a partner and practice the dialogues below.

⭐ Task 1

A ：　請問你找哪一位？
zhǎo　nǎ　　wèi

B ：　我找謝小明。
wǒ zhǎo

A ：　好，請你等一下。
děng yí xià

B ：　謝謝！

⭐ Task 2

A ：　請問你找哪一位？
zhǎo nǎ　　wèi

B ：　我找小明的爸爸。
zhǎo

A ：　他不在家。

⭐ Task 3

A ：　你好，請問你找誰？
zhǎo shéi

B ：　我找大關。
zhǎo

A ：　對不起，大關不在家。

Go 100

WANT TO LEARN MORE?

Check out the Text > Dialogue section in the Go100 CD.

Task 4

Ⓐ 你好，請問小明在家嗎？

Ⓑ děng yí xià
請你等一下。

dǎ diàn huà zhǎo
哥哥，有人打電話找你。

Task 5

Ⓐ 你好，我是小明，我要找大關。
zhǎo

Ⓑ 對不起，大關不在家。

Ⓐ 明天他在家嗎？

Ⓑ 明天他在家。

Ⓐ dǎ diàn huà zhǎo
明天我再打電話找他。

Task 6

Ⓐ diàn huà   hào
請問你家電話是幾號？

Ⓑ diàn huà
我家電話是27507631。

It is 5:00p.m. on a Wednesday. You are watching television with your brother when the telephone rings. Your brother answers the call.

 Group discussion

Based on clues from your brother's dialogue, write down what you think the caller is saying. You missed some parts of the conversation because the television was too loud. Discuss with your group members and complete your brother's dialogue.

These key phrases may be useful in your discussion:

哥哥 / 媽媽 / 爸爸 / 弟弟　　現在 / 早上 / 下午 / 早一點兒 / 晚一點兒
下午四點鐘 / 下午六點鐘 / 早上十點鐘 / 中午十二點鐘
我是…… /你是…… /他是…… /朋友

哥哥：你好！請問你找哪一位？
caller:
哥哥：她現在不在家，請你（＿＿＿＿＿＿＿）再打來。
caller:
哥哥：現在下午五點鐘，請你（＿＿＿＿＿＿＿）再打來。
caller:
哥哥：請問你是哪一位？
caller:
哥哥：再見。

② After completing the conversation, find a partner and role-play the scenario. Take turns to play the role of the brother and the caller.

LEARNING LOG

I can...

		Excellent	Good	Fair	Needs Improvement
1	ask the caller who he/she is looking for as well as say who I am looking for in a phone conversation.	✓			
2	respond appropriately after the caller identifies who he/she is looking for.		✓		
3	inquire about and tell the telephone number.			✓	
4	tell the difference between "那" and "哪".				✓
5	write "找", "誰", "打", "話", and "來".	✓			

好老師
A Good Teacher

My Goals

1 Be able to ask about or say the things I (or others) know about
2 Be able to ask about or say the things I (or others) can do
3 Know how to address the teacher in Chinese
4 Learn vocabulary associated with expressing my abilities

Let's
READ

lǎo shī
老師好！

tóng xué
同學好！

lǎo shī
我是王老師，

jiāo   zhōng wén
今天教你們中文，

yì qǐ xué zhōng wén
我們一起學中文。

TIP How do you address your teachers? Chinese people address their teachers as "(teacher's last name) + 老師", for example, "王老師". This is different from "Mr. Wang" or "Ms. Wang" in English, which in Chinese means "王先生" and "王小姐" respectively.

lǎo   shī
老 師

New Words

lǎo shī 老師 teacher	xué 學 to learn	tóng xué 同學 classmate	jiāo 教 to teach
zhōng wén 中文 the Chinese language		yì qǐ 一起 together	

jiāo

教

xué

學

lǎo shī jiāo
老師教我。

lǎo shī jiāo zhōng wén
老師教我中文。

lǎo shī jiāo xué zhōng wén
老師教我學中文。

xué zhōng wén
我學中文。

xué zhōng wén
我們學中文。

yì qǐ xué zhōng wén
我們一起學中文。

lǎo shī jiāo zhōng wén
老師教我們中文。

lǎo shī jiāo xué zhōng wén
老師教我們學中文。

lǎo shī jiāo xué zhōng wén
謝謝老師教我們學中文。

xué shēng xué zhōng wén yǒu yòng
學生：學中文有用嗎？

lǎo shī xué zhōng wén yǒu yòng
老師：學中文很有用。

New Words

xué shēng
學生　student; pupil

yǒu yòng
有用　useful

好老師　103

lǎo shī　　　tóng xué
老師好，同學好。

lǎo shī jiāo　　xué zhōng wén
老師教我學中文。

hé tóng xué yì qǐ xué
我和同學一起學，

huì kě yǐ　　lǎo shī
不會可以問老師。

New Words

hé
和 and; with; together with

huì
會 be able to; can

kě yǐ
可以 may; can

Let's Learn GRAMMAR

huì / huì
會 / 不會

| 我 | huì 會 / huì 不會 | zhōng wén 中文。 |

huì zhōng wén
我會中文。

huì　　　　zhōng wén
我會一點兒中文。

huì zhōng wén
我不會中文。

huì zhōng wén　　　　　　huì　rì　wén
哥哥會中文，他不會日文(Japanese)。

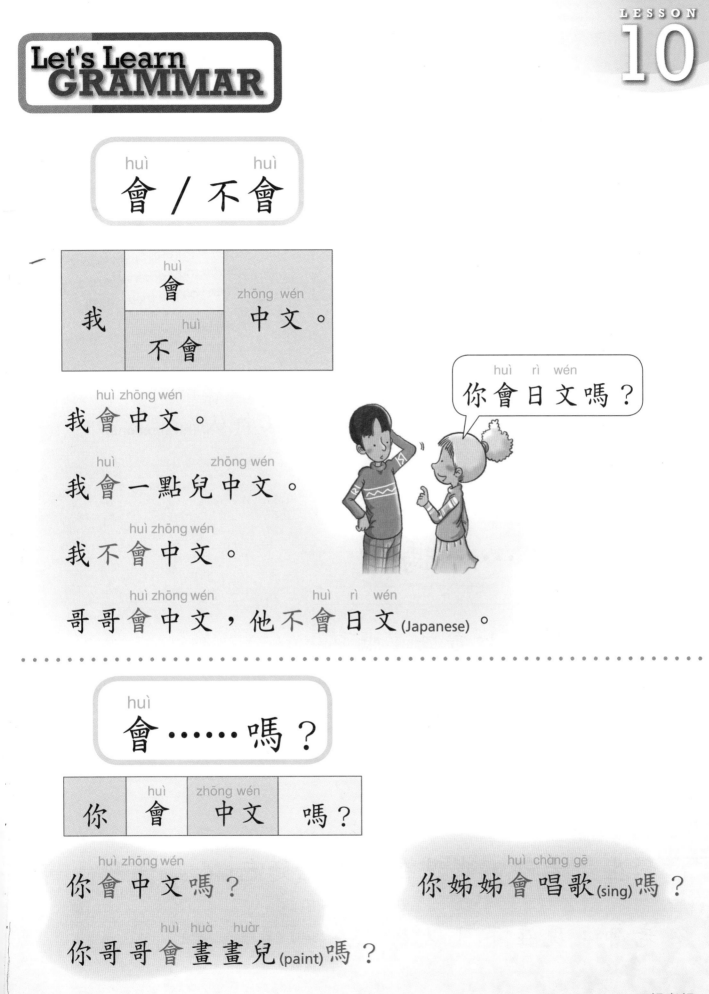

huì　rì　wén
你會日文嗎？

huì
會……嗎？

| 你 | huì 會 | zhōng wén 中文 | 嗎？ |

huì zhōng wén
你會中文嗎？

huì huà huàr
你哥哥會畫畫兒(paint)嗎？

huì chàng gē
你姊姊會唱歌(sing)嗎？

可以 / 不可以
(kě yǐ / kě yǐ)

你	可以 (kě yǐ) / 不可以 (kě yǐ)	打電話。

TIP

"可以" and "不可以" may become an imperative in certain phrases or sentences, so you must observe your tone when you use these words.

你可以來我家。
(kě yǐ)

他可以打電話。
(kě yǐ)

你不可以打人(hit someone)。
(kě yǐ dǎ rén)

可以……嗎？
(kě yǐ)

我	可以 (kě yǐ)	打電話	嗎？

我可以學中文嗎？
(kě yǐ xué zhōng wén)

明天下午，我可以來嗎？
(kě yǐ)

學生：老師，我現在可以吃麵包(eat bread)嗎？
(xué shēng) (lǎo shī) (kě yǐ chī miàn bāo)

老師：現在不可以。
(lǎo shī) (kě yǐ)

yì qǐ
一起

yì qǐ xué zhōng wén
我們一起學中文。

hé yì qǐ shàng xué
我和哥哥一起去上學(go to school)。

hé tóng xué yì qǐ tī zú qiú
我和同學一起踢足球(play soccer)。

yì qǐ
妹妹等姊姊一起走。

zhōng wén
中文。

xué zhōng wén
學中文。

yì qǐ xué zhōng wén
一起學中文。

hé yì qǐ xué zhōng wén
我和弟弟一起學中文。

hé yì qǐ xué zhōng wén
星期六我和弟弟一起學中文。

Go 100

WANT TO LEARN MORE?

Check out the Text > Sentence Pattern section in the Go100 CD.

Find a partner. Practice and create the dialogues below.

⭐ Task 1

Ⓐ 請問你會中文嗎？
huì zhōng wén

Ⓑ 我會一點兒。你會中文嗎？
huì huì zhōng wén

Ⓐ 我會中文。
huì zhōng wén

Ⓑ 你姊姊會中文嗎？
huì zhōng wén

Ⓐ 她會，她教我中文，她是我的中文老師。
huì jiāo zhōng wén zhōng wén lǎo shī

Ⓑ 你會日文嗎？
huì rì wén

Ⓐ 我不會，我不會日文。
huì huì rì wén

⭐ Task 2

錢 鐘 話 問 們
同 用 弟 半 關

Ⓐ 這十個字，你會幾個字？
zì huì zì

Ⓑ 我會＿＿＿＿＿＿。
huì

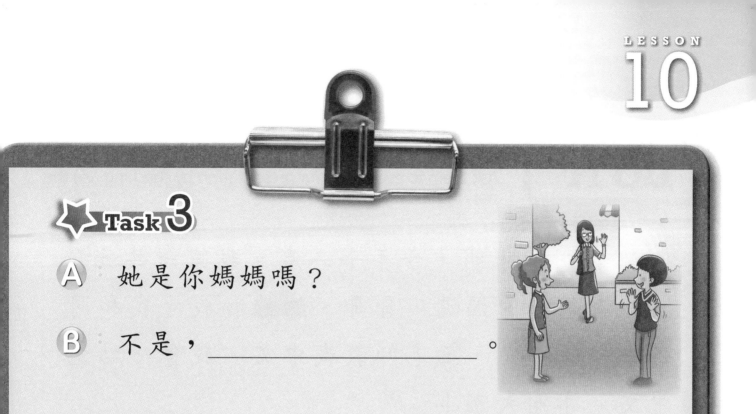

Task 3

Ⓐ 她是你媽媽嗎？

Ⓑ 不是，＿＿＿＿＿＿＿＿＿＿＿＿。

Task 4

kě yǐ

Ⓐ 我可以問你嗎？

Ⓑ 你要問什麼？

Ⓐ ＿＿＿＿＿＿＿＿＿＿？

Ⓑ ＿＿＿＿＿＿＿＿＿＿。

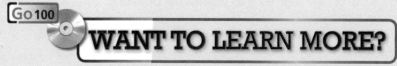

Check out the Text > Dialogue section in the Go100 CD.

Let's DO IT

Do a self-introduction in class. Rewrite your introduction based on the text below, and read it to your teacher and classmates. Ask them to evaluate your presentation by checking (✓) the stars in the table.

我叫謝小明，今年~~十~~歲。我家一共~~五口~~，有爸爸、媽媽、哥哥、~~弟弟~~和我。我和同學一起學中文，~~○○~~老師教我中文，我會一點兒中文。謝謝大家！

Evaluator	Score
Myself	⭐⭐⭐ 3
Teacher	⭐⭐ 2
Friend	⭐ 1
Parents	⭐⭐⭐ 3

LEARNING LOG

I can...	Excellent	Good	Fair	Needs Improvement
1 use "會" and "會……嗎？" correctly to talk about what I can do or ask others about their abilities.				☒
2 use "可以" and "會" correctly to express my opinions.				☒
3 tell the difference between the usage of "教" and "學" and use them correctly.			☒	
4 tell the difference between addressing the teacher in English and Chinese.	☒	☒		
5 write "和", "學", "會", "可", and "以".	☒			

Vocabulary Index

Pinyin	Bopomofo	Traditional Character	English	Simplified Character	Lesson
B					
bā	ㄅㄚ	八	eight		L1
bà	ㄅㄚˋ	爸	father		L6
bǎi	ㄅㄞˇ	百	hundred		L1
bàn	ㄅㄢˋ	半	half		L8
bú kè qì	ㄅㄨˊ ㄎㄜˋ ㄑㄧˋ	不客氣	you're welcome	不客气	L3
bú yòng	ㄅㄨˊ ㄩㄥˋ	不用	no need		L3
D					
dà	ㄉㄚˋ	大	big		L5
dǎ diàn huà	ㄉㄚˇ ㄉㄧㄢˋ ㄏㄨㄚˋ	打電話	to make a phone call	打电话	L9
dà jiā	ㄉㄚˋ ㄐㄧㄚ	大家	everybody		L2
dào	ㄉㄠˋ	到	to arrive		L5
de	ㄉㄜ˙	的	(particle before a noun)		L4
děng yì děng	ㄉㄥˇ ㄧˋ ㄉㄥˇ	等一等	wait a moment	等一等	L9
dì	ㄉㄧˋ	弟	younger brother		L6
diǎn	ㄉㄧㄢˇ	點	o'clock (indicating time of day)	点	L8
...diǎn zhōng	……ㄉㄧㄢˇ ㄓㄨㄥ	……點鐘	o'clock (indicating time of day)	……点钟	L8
dōu	ㄉㄡ	都	all; already		L4
duì bù qǐ	ㄉㄨㄟˋ ㄅㄨˋ ㄑㄧˇ	對不起	sorry	对不起	L3
duō shǎo	ㄉㄨㄛ ㄕㄠˇ	多少	how many; how much		L7
E					
èr	ㄦˋ	二	two		L1
F					
fēn	ㄈㄣ	分	minute		L8
fēn zhōng	ㄈㄣ ㄓㄨㄥ	分鐘	minute	分钟	L8
G					
gē	ㄍㄜ	哥	older brother		L6
gè	ㄍㄜˋ	個	(a measure word, used for objects and people)	个	L1
guì	ㄍㄨㄟˋ	貴	expensive	贵	L7
guì xìng	ㄍㄨㄟˋ ㄒㄧㄥˋ	貴姓	last name (formal)	贵姓	L4
H					
hái yǒu	ㄏㄞˊ ㄧㄡˇ	還有	still; also; and	还有	L6

hǎo	ㄏㄠˇ	好	fine; good		L2
hào	ㄏㄠˋ	號	number	号	L9
hé	ㄏㄜˊ	和	and; with; together with		L10
hěn	ㄏㄣˇ	很	very		L2
huì	ㄏㄨㄟˋ	會	be able to; can	会	L10

J

jǐ	ㄐㄧˇ	幾	which; how many; a few	几	L5
jiā	ㄐㄧㄚ	家	home; family		L6
jiāo	ㄐㄧㄠ	教	to teach		L10
jiào	ㄐㄧㄠˋ	叫	to call		L4
jiě	ㄐㄧㄝˇ	姊	older sister	姐	L6
jīn nián	ㄐㄧㄣ ㄋㄧㄢˊ	今年	this year		L5
jīn tiān	ㄐㄧㄣ ㄊㄧㄢ	今天	today		L5
jiǔ	ㄐㄧㄡˇ	九	nine		L1

K

kě yǐ	ㄎㄜˇ ㄧˇ	可以	may; can	可以	L10
kǒu	ㄎㄡˇ	口	(a measure word used for counting family members)		L6
kuài	ㄎㄨㄞˋ	塊	(unit of currency)	块	L7

L

lái	ㄌㄞˊ	來	to come	来	L9
lǎo shī	ㄌㄠˇ ㄕ	老師	teacher	老师	L10
liǎng	ㄌㄧㄤˇ	兩	two	两	L1
liù	ㄌㄧㄡˋ	六	six		L1

M

mā	ㄇㄚ	媽	mother	妈	L6
ma	ㄇㄚ˙	嗎	(used when asking a question)	吗	L2
mǎi	ㄇㄞˇ	買	buy	买	L7
mèi	ㄇㄟˋ	妹	younger sister		L6
méi guān xi	ㄇㄟˊ ㄍㄨㄢ ㄒㄧ˙	沒關係	it's fine	没关系	L3
míng nián	ㄇㄧㄥˊ ㄋㄧㄢˊ	明年	next year		L5
míng tiān	ㄇㄧㄥˊ ㄊㄧㄢ	明天	tomorrow		L5
míng zi	ㄇㄧㄥˊ ㄗ˙	名字	name; first name		L4

N

nǎ	ㄋㄚˇ	哪	which; what		L9
nà ge	ㄋㄚˋ ㄍㄜ˙	那個	that	那个	L7

nǐ	ㄋㄧˇ	你	you (singular)		L2
nǐ hǎo	ㄋㄧˇ ㄏㄠˇ	你好	hello		L2
nǐ men	ㄋㄧˇ ㄇㄣ•	你們	you (plural)	你们	L2
nǐ zǎo	ㄋㄧˇ ㄗㄠˇ	你早	Good morning (to you)		L2
nián	ㄋㄧㄢˊ	年	year		L5

P

pián yí	ㄆㄧㄢˊ ㄧˊ	便宜	cheap		L7

Q

qī	ㄑㄧ	七	seven		L1
qián	ㄑㄧㄢˊ	錢	money	钱	L7
qǐng	ㄑㄧㄥˇ	請	please; invite	请	L3
qǐng wèn	ㄑㄧㄥˇ ㄨㄣˋ	請問	may I ask	请问	L4
qù nián	ㄑㄩˋ ㄋㄧㄢˊ	去年	last year		L5

R

rén	ㄖㄣˊ	人	people; human beings		L6
rì	ㄖˋ	日	day; date		L5

S

sān	ㄙㄢ	三	three		L1
shàng wǔ	ㄕㄤˋ ㄨˇ	上午	morning		L8
shén me	ㄕㄣˊ ㄇㄜ•	什麼	what	什么	L4
shí	ㄕˊ	十	ten		L1
shí	ㄕˊ	時	time; when	时	L8
shì	ㄕˋ	是	to be (am, are, is)		L5
shéi	ㄕㄟˊ	誰	who; whom	谁	L9
sì	ㄙˋ	四	four		L1
suàn	ㄙㄨㄢˋ	算	to calculate or count		L7
suì	ㄙㄨㄟˋ	歲	years of age (a measure word)	岁	L7

T

tā	ㄊㄚ	他	he; him		L2
tā	ㄊㄚ	她	she; her		L3
tā men	ㄊㄚ ㄇㄣ•	他們	they; them	他们	L2
tài guì le	ㄊㄞˋ ㄍㄨㄟˋ ㄌㄜ•	太貴了	too expensive	太贵了	L7
tiān	ㄊㄧㄢ	天	day; sky		L5
tóng xué	ㄊㄨㄥˊ ㄒㄩㄝˊ	同學	classmate	同学	L10

W

wǎn shàng	ㄨㄢˇ ㄕㄤˋ	晚上	night		L8

wáng	ㄨㄤˊ	王	(a Chinese last name)			L4
wèi	ㄨㄟˋ	位	(a measure word for people)			L9
wǒ	ㄨㄛˇ	我	I			L2
wǒ men	ㄨㄛˇ ㄇㄣ˙	我們	we; us		我们	L2
wǔ	ㄨˇ	五	five			L1
X						
xià wǔ	ㄒㄧㄚˋ ㄨˇ	下午	afternoon			L8
xiàn zài	ㄒㄧㄢˋ ㄗㄞˋ	現在	now		现在	L8
xiǎo	ㄒㄧㄠˇ	小	small; little			L5
xiǎo guì	ㄒㄧㄠˇ ㄍㄨㄟˋ	小貴	(a Chinese name)		小贵	L4
xiǎo míng	ㄒㄧㄠˇ ㄇㄧㄥˊ	小明	(a Chinese name)			L4
xiè xie	ㄒㄧㄝˋ ㄒㄧㄝ˙	謝謝	thank you		谢谢	L3
xìng	ㄒㄧㄥˋ	姓	last name			L4
xīng qí	ㄒㄧㄥ ㄑㄧˊ	星期	week			L5
xué	ㄒㄩㄝˊ	學	to learn		学	L10
xué shēng	ㄒㄩㄝˊ ㄕㄥ	學生	student; pupil		学生	L10
Y						
yào	ㄧㄠˋ	要	need; want			L7
yī	ㄧ	一	one			L1
yì diǎnr	ㄧˋ ㄉㄧㄢˇ ㄦ	一點兒	a little bit		一点儿	L7
yí gòng	ㄧˊ ㄍㄨㄥˋ	一共	in total			L6
yì qǐ	ㄧˋ ㄑㄧˇ	一起	together			L10
yǒu	ㄧㄡˇ	有	have			L5
yǒu yòng	ㄧㄡˇ ㄩㄥˋ	有用	useful			L10
yuè	ㄩㄝˋ	月	month			L5
Z						
zài	ㄗㄞˋ	在	in			L8
zài jiàn	ㄗㄞˋ ㄐㄧㄢˋ	再見	goodbye		再见	L2
zǎo	ㄗㄠˇ	早	early; morning			L2
zhǎo	ㄓㄠˇ	找	to look for; to find			L9
zhè ge	ㄓㄜˋ ㄍㄜ˙	這個	this		这个	L5
zhōng wén	ㄓㄨㄥ ㄨㄣˊ	中文	the Chinese language			L10
zhōng wǔ	ㄓㄨㄥ ㄨˇ	中午	noon			L8
zǒu	ㄗㄡˇ	走	depart; walk; leave			L8
zuó tiān	ㄗㄨㄛˊ ㄊㄧㄢ	昨天	yesterday			L5